rland E

ing Gazette

Test

on

(NY)

C000179103

Heartbreak̲ı̲n̲g̲ ̲T̲e̲s̲t̲

THREE BATS THAT FLASHED

BRADMAN

AMES

VERITY

Verity also made several fine sweeps
to leg off Wall and then Ames had
another go at Bradman in the next over.
A hard drive through covers to the
boundary gave Ames his 50 after he had
batted 2 hours 19 minutes. He repeated
the shot off the next ball.
Altogether 11 were scored off the over,
Ames claiming ten and Verity one.

McCABE TRIED

This rough handling of Bradman forced
Woodfull to take him off at 376.
McCabe was the new bowler, but he
failed to bring about a separation, and
when lunch was taken the score was 385
for 6—Ames 64 and Verity 36.
The stand has so far yielded 89 and
increased England's lead to 504.
During the interval it was revealed that
Richardson missed a very hard chance of
catching Verity off Wall when 25. Ironmonger, who opened the bowling from the
river end when play was resumed, bowled
round the wicket for the first time in
the match.

He had three slips, a point, cover, extra
cover, and mid-off. O'Reilly was on at
the other end. Ames and Verity went
through the process of playing themselves
in again and play was once more on the
dull side, one run being scored in ten

SIGNS OF BETTER TIMES

"Even" in County Durham"

COL. HEADLAM PRAISES TARIFFS

Colonel Cuthbert Headlam, M.P., speak-
ing at Barnard Castle last night, said
that although the system of tariffs might
not have worked miracles, it had had a
great effect upon our national position,
financial and economical. Since the
Exchequer had gained the sum of 30
millions of new revenue as a result he
failed to see how anyone could object to it.
Tariffs had been adopted only for the
purpose of bargaining with the foreigner.
It was surely worth the effort to have
raised 30 millions of new revenue without
increasing the price to the consumer of
the articles taxed.

NATION'S REVENUE FIGURES

Balance to be Made Up

INCOME-TAX SPURT NEEDED

From April 1 to January 14 ordinary
revenue of the country was £437,550,851.
Last year at this time the ordinary
revenue was £474,066,857, a difference of
£16,516,006. The estimate for the year is
£766,800,000, so that by March 31 there is
a balance of £309,249,149 to be made up.
Income-tax receipts last week were
£18,644,000. From April 1, 1932, to
January 14, 1933, the income-tax receipts
were £96,701,000, against £126,225,000
from April 1, 1931, to January 14 last
year.
The estimated total for the year

A Cuckoo in the Bodyline Nest

A Cuckoo
in the
Bodyline Nest

Gilbert Mant

Kangaroo Press

© Gilbert Mant 1992

First published in 1992 by Kangaroo Press Pty Ltd
3 Whitehall Road (P.O. Box 75) Kenthurst NSW 2156
Typeset by G.T. Setters Pty Limited
Printed by Southwood Press Pty Ltd, Marrickville

ISBN 0 86417 490 X

Contents

Acknowledgments

I am indebted to Jack Pollard, OAM, that indefatigable cricket writer and researcher, for making available photographs from his extensive collection for this book. Included in them are some memorable action pictures from the old-fashioned camera of Bert Fishwick, who followed the 1932–33 Tests for the *Sydney Morning Herald* with Tom Goodman, its able cricket reporter.

A bibliography on another page contains a list of some of the many books I read, or re-read, to refresh my memory of events that took place sixty years ago and to quote the reactions, then and afterwards, of the main characters in the bodyline drama. If people with sharp eyes recognise a section very like a chapter about Sydney journalism in the 1920s in J.H. Fingleton's 1981 autobiography, *Batting From Memory* (Collins, London and Sydney), it is not plagiarism; I was commissioned by him to write it and he made his acknowledgment. 'The Night the Ambassadors Caught on Fire' (see Chapter 2) first appeared in a literary supplement of the Sydney *Bulletin*.

I have to thank my son, Alistair Mant, of Brighton, England, for researching British reaction and newspaper coverage of the bodyline affair in 1932–33. For this, he enlisted the support of Sir Richard Storey, Bt., chairman of Portsmouth and Sunderland Newspapers plc and former chairman of the U.K. Press Association Council. The researches of Sir Richard and his colleagues were of immense value to me in background information and I am truly grateful to them. I thank also David Frith, eminent English cricket writer and editor of *Wisden Cricket Monthly*, for his encouragement.

I feel guilty about sending my cousin, Mrs Tommy Lown, on a reconnoitre of the seventy-six steps of Breakneck Steps in Darling Point when I might have been born at the top of a different set of steps in a different suburb of Sydney. And I thank Yvonne Bartlett Hawes for typing the manuscript of the book and helping with its production in so many other ways. I thank, too, Carl Harrison-Ford, my Kangaroo Press editor, for his sound advice. If I have left anybody out, you must blame it on lapses of my nonagenarian memory.

Gilbert Mant

1

Breakneck Steps

I've lived through three Great Wars, acting as a war correspondent in two of them. There was World War I of 1914–18, World War II of 1939–45 and in between them the Great Cricket Bodyline War of 1932–33.

This book is what can loosely be described as yet another 'inside story' of the Bodyline War. I am the sole survivor of the press corps who travelled with the English team from first ball to last ball, eight long months as a camp follower. It was a war that nearly split the British Empire and made Australia a republic long before its time. It is now sixty years after the outbreak of hostilities and still the interest in it by old and young is phenomenal. Countless books, documentaries, film and television features have been produced on the subject. One Australian TV mini-series was notable for being riddled with mistakes and inaccuracies.

When you reach the age of ninety, as I have at the time of this writing, you are often asked to nominate the greatest events that have occurred during your lifetime. Bodyline would certainly be in my top twenty. I suppose World Wars I and II and the development of atomic power would head my list. The others would include the contraceptive pill, which revolutionised moral and sexual standards; the legal removal of the stigma of illegitimacy; the commercialisation of the noble and gracious game of cricket by Kerry Packer; the first man on the moon; women's liberation; the decline in public respect for the professions of law, medicine and schoolteaching.

I've sired two children, been married twice, served in the

ranks as an infantryman, survived shot, shell and bomb as a war correspondent, travelled around the world half a dozen times and had eleven books published.

These things, momentous to me as a meek and timid person, have dominated my life, yet it is the bodyline tour that singles me out from my fellows.

'You know, Gilbert travelled with the Poms during the bodyline tour,' acquaintances proudly introduce me to strangers.

In a moment I am the centre of attention. 'What was Jardine *really* like?' 'Did Maurice Tate really hit him over the head with a beer bottle?' 'Were the Poms really trying to kill Bradman?' 'What did you think of bodyline yourself?'

I am undeservedly regarded as an oracle on all things pertaining to the game of cricket and am listened to with great respect. I give weighty opinions on the performances of present-day cricketers, on the intricacies of spin bowling and tactics on the field. I am not backward in expressing my dislike of the one-day pyjama games—I believe they destroy the true art and soul of cricket and have ruined many a promising player. If the truth were known, my opinions are generally worthless but deep down I enjoy the notoriety.

There are no great revelations in this book but I can say in all seriousness that the bodyline controversy would have taken an entirely different course if somebody other than I had been the Reuter representative with the English team. I still feel a bit guilty about it and I shall explain it all as we go along. My association with it was the culmination of a number of lucky factors.

In a sort of a way my link with bodyline goes back to eleven days after my birth on 20 July 1902, in Marathon Avenue, Darling Point, Sydney. The next-door neighbours, the Allens, were blessed with the birth of George Oswald Browning Allen on 31 July in that same year. Both our fathers were lawyers.

(I have some awkward explaining to do here. Pre-publication extracts from this book appeared earlier this year in *Wisden Cricket Monthly* (England), including the occasion of my birth in Marathon Avenue. It was some months later before I became aware of E.W. Swanton's biography, *Gubby Allen: Man of Cricket* (Hutchinson/Stanley Paul, London). It was a shock to read that Gubby attributed his birthplace as being a house built by his father in Victoria Road, Bellevue Hill, another suburb of Sydney. I am at a loss to explain this contradiction, as Gubby and I both accepted and talked about our next-door-neighbour relationship in later life. Perhaps some other Allens lived next door in Marathon Avenue or perhaps I was born in Victoria Road. Who knows and does it really matter ninety years later?)

Marathon Avenue was then a short street at the top of the aptly named Breakneck Steps, leading precipitously down to William Street in Double Bay. It seemed to me that there were hundreds of steps to be negotiated, a difficult task for a child, both descending and ascending. (The steps are still there and a recent reconnoitre by my cousin, Mrs Tommy Lown, confirmed that there are actually only seventy-six steps. The Woollahra Council told her they were not aware that the steps once had a name. It is not too late for them to restore it with a suitable signpost.)

Those were the days of gaslight and hansom cabs. Big events in childhood included periodical visits to the neighbourhood by an Italian organ-grinder and his monkey, a German band, and an aged and wrinkled Chinese gardener carrying his vegetables across his shoulders with a bamboo pole. There was always the gift of a jar of ginger at Christmas time.

I can't really recall George Oswald Browning Allen as a childhood playmate and there were few parallels in our lives, apart from being born in the same street within 11 days of each other.

G.O.B. Allen was taken away from Australia to live in England with his parents at about the age of six. He went to Eton and Cambridge, became captain of England at cricket, chairman of the MCC (Marylebone Cricket Club not the Melbourne Cricket Club), a successful London stockbroker and ultimately accepted a knighthood as Sir George Allen. At the time of the Bodyline War, Gubby was a member of the English touring party.

On my part, I was the black sheep of the Mant family by becoming a journalist. I did, however, attend Sydney Grammar School and reach the dizzy heights of captaining the Sydney Journalists' Club cricket team. I did not get to England for the first time until I was nineteen years old and, alas, never became Sir Gilbert.

My path to becoming Reuters cricket representative was about as tortuous as the ups and downs of Breakneck Steps. I was taken away from school at the age of sixteen when the family doctor said I would have to get away from the sea air of Sydney to a dry climate. So I was dumped off a train at a railway siding with the almost unspellable, unpronounceable name of Mullengudgery, between Warren and Nyngan in western New South Wales.

Those smart Sydney doctors knew a thing or two about dry climates. It was mid-summer at Mullengudgery and it had not rained for nearly two years in one of the worst droughts in history. My two years as a jackeroo on Eenaweena Station certainly got rid of the sea air in my system. For weeks the temperature stuck in the 100s, once reaching a record 120 degrees Fahrenheit in the shade. Day after day the hot winds swept across the western plains under a brassy sun. Suffocating dust rose from the brown, bare earth, and dizzy, endless lines of fences stretched across the paddocks until they flickered into the mirages.

We three 'gentlemen' jackaroos were the slave labour of the station. We were paid ten shillings a week for the doubtful privilege of living at the homestead instead of in the station hands' quarters. We worked a hard and long day on horseback, mustering and trying to keep alive the remaining valuable Merino sheep on the stud property.

There was practically no grass or herbage left, so we had to turn to the trees for feed. We systematically lopped the green branches from every tree on the station—wilga, mulga, leopardwood, brigalow. It was back-breaking work in the blazing heat. We perched precariously on the limbs of edible trees and hacked right-handed and left-handed with our small axes at the branches for twelve hours a day.

Battalions of black ants were shaken down our necks; regiments of flies and mosquitoes assailed us; and sometimes we disturbed hives of vicious wild bees. The starving sheep clustered beneath us, ravenously licking up the green leaves and branches as fast as they fell to the ground.

We dried up like parchment or raisins in the searing sun. The lack of green vegetables and fresh water gave us a kind of scurvy, locally known as 'Barcoo rot'. Our skins literally rotted and I had a sudden sympathy for the ancient mariners of old England. Any kind of graze ripped the flesh from our hands. The sores festered horribly and we struggled to do our work swathed in bandages. Some of us had an epidemic of boils. I still bear the scar where a drunken doctor in Warren lanced a boil on the side of my throat. I thought my end had come as the scalpel shook crazily in his hand.

This was the sort of life we gentlemen jackaroos lived. It should have soured me forever for life in the bush, but it didn't. (I suppose jackaroos live in the lap of luxury these days, with fat award salaries.) The war was still on and I tried to get away from it all by offering to enlist in the army as a bugler. The army did not need buglers, it seemed, and in any case I did not know how to blow a bugle.

One thing about my life as a jackaroo that eventually led me to become a Bodyline War Correspondent was a sudden urge to write. I began churning out bush verses and short articles for a popular weekly publication of the time, the *Town and Country Journal*. The editor of the young peoples' pages was 'Dame Durden', who gave me great encouragement and advice. It was years before I discovered that my mentor had been Ethel Turner of *Seven Little Australians* fame.

World War I ended in 1918 and I said goodbye to Mullengudgery, carrying the blotches of Barcoo rot and scars of various surgeons' scalpels that are with me to this day. Cooma was my headquarters for the next seven or eight years, engaged in jackarooing, rabbit trapping and various other rural pursuits.

At some stage of the game, a bit of luck came my way. I inherited some money from the estate of my grandfather, George Mant, a grazing and cattle pioneer of the Maryborough district of Queensland. Grandfather Mant settled there in 1856 and raised a large family, of whom my father, William Hall Mant, was the youngest son. When the Mant inheritance came, I was working as a jackaroo for my dear friend, Tom Knox, on Cania, a property to the south of Cooma. In a share-farming deal with Tom, I used my inheritance to fence, plough and sow a crop of potatoes on five acres of his land. The crop was a bonanza and, on the spur of the moment, I shot off to England with my friends, the Connors (the cost of a sea passage to Southampton in those days was a mere £50).

The urge for a career in writing or journalism burned fiercely in me at the time and I dreamed of storming Fleet Street in London. By then I had had some success in Sydney publications with verses, short stories and articles. I sailed off in high hopes.

I soon discovered that Fleet Street was not an easy street to storm for a young unknown Australian freelance writer. I had a reasonable amount of work accepted by London editors but it was not enough to live on, even in a garret. After twelve months I had just enough money left to cable two words to my brother, John, a Sydney lawyer: 'Broke Gilbert'. Brother John came good with enough money to take me home. Someday I would try again.

2

The Fourth Estate

It was 1924. I was twenty-two years of age and going nowhere fast. The family were worried about me. Brother John tried vainly to find me another jackarooing job.

In the meantime, I kept at my writing, with some success with *The Bulletin*, then an influential political and literary weekly. But it was an aimless existence, not alleviated when I published a small volume of verse and prose at my own expense. It is a literary axiom that an aspiring writer should never, never do this kind of thing. In the trade, it is known as 'vanity publishing'. I printed 250 copies, of which I gave away fifty. The public bought seventeen copies and the rest were 'remaindered', or got rid of. The one bright spot in this debacle was a review in the Sydney *Daily Telegraph* by Alec H. Chisholm, one of Australia's most noted ornithologists, editors and author of many books. He intimated that my book was pretty awful in parts but that it would be 'churlish' not to recognise the underlying talent of the writer. Good old Chis! A year or so later, that review was to prove the pundits wrong and set me well on the path to bodyline.

(I retain a slightly lecherous recollection of Alec Chisholm some thirty years later when he was editing a new edition of the *Australian Encyclopaedia* from a second floor office of Angus and Robertson, booksellers, of Castlereagh Street, Sydney. I called to see him and he led me over to the window facing the David Jones store on the opposite side of the street. 'As a well-known pervert, Gilly,' he said in his usual sardonic manner. 'What do you see over there?' I looked across and straight into the fitting-rooms of the ladies' underwear department where some very attractive females were striking poses in various states of undress. Chis confessed that he found the sight very distracting when he was trying to edit an article on boll weevil in wheat for inclusion in the encyclopaedia under the letter 'W'.)

After the disaster of my book I decided to get out of the city and gravitated back to Cooma. Thus began a preposterous period of my life when I became a rabbit-trapper and, later, a rabbit skin buyer in partnership with the wildest Irishman I have ever encountered.

I trapped rabbits with a Cooma man named Blyton in the hills near Adaminaby in the depth of winter. It was in sharp contrast with the blistering heat of Mullengudgery and I can't recall whether we ever made much money out of it. The local paper described our efforts as 'an expedition undertaken with the assistance of borrowed horse and buggy, on which were packed or hung bedding, clothes, food, traps, lanterns and kerosene tin buckets, the whole contraption being guaranteed to frighten every rabbit for miles into the farthest recess of its burrow'.

It was after this abortive attempt to make my fortune that Tiernan Thomas O'Rourke, descendant of the Kings of Ireland, came into my life. I first met Terry O'Rourke when he arrived in Cooma with a price on his head, so he said, and a pension from the British government. For Terry was a Black and Tan. He told horrible stories of savagery by both sides during The Trouble in Ireland.

A small, slim man, he limped from a wound in the 1914–18 war and there was a large hole in the back of his neck where an Irish gunman had got him with a forty-four in the bar of a Dublin hotel. Terry retaliated, in his own words, by firing his own gun and 'scattering his brains all over the bar'. He still packed an incredible armoury of lethal weapons—a couple of revolvers, a rifle, a shotgun and a sabre. He had an idea that 'They' were after him and he wasn't taking any chances. He would have been a prominent member of today's gun lobby.

We had very little money between us but we formed O'Rourke, Mant & Co., surely the most bizarre company in history. We bought a T-model (1914) Ford car and made raids into the surrounding countryside, buying rabbit skins, sheep skins, hides, dead wool, tallow, hooves and empty bottles. We slept among the stinking things at night in the old Cooma drill hall. We acquired a third conspirator, a young Yorkshireman named Jack Critchley, who was more interested in girls than rabbit skins.

The operation of our company, without any money to speak of, was absurdly simple. We made an arrangement with a big Sydney skin and produce firm, who staked us for our first consignment of skins, hides *et al.*, and then gave us a percentage per pound on all subsequent purchases. The only trouble was that we were always in debt for the initial grubstake and in the end we went broke.

I remember crazy car drives in our T-model Ford from Cooma to Adaminaby, with Terry firing off his revolver at the tin mail boxes on gateposts and singing 'Kathleen Mavoureen' in a soft falsetto. He could write his name on a wall with revolver bullets and one night put a bullet through a blacksmith's hat near Cooma Creek. The blacksmith was wearing it at the time.

We knew every pub, every road, every bush track on the Monaro, from Kiandra to Adaminaby, Jindabyne, Berridale, Cooma, Nimmitabel and down over the Brown Mountain to the South Coast. There, Terry sold cars to unsuspecting cockies, teaching them to drive in the paddocks. We were always going to make our fortunes—but we never did.

Terry had the blarney. He spoke rapidly and broke into Gaelic songs every now and then. He had rabbit-trappers out in the mountains gaping at his tales of Ireland. One day we bought skins from a big young Englishman who was distinctly 'different'. We put him down as a remittance man or something equally mysterious. Next time we went to his camp we discovered he had moved on and we forgot about him. More than ten years later, at a diplomatic function in Ottawa, I was aware of something familiar about a big man among the guests.

I whispered to him, 'Do you know anything about trapping rabbits?' He looked at me in amazement and then we laughed together. The man in question had lived in the south of France for many years and after that meeting we corresponded spasmodically. He wrote under the name of Stephen Lister and was the author of countless bestsellers. In his last letter to me he said he received a surprising amount of fan mail from Australia, though none of his books had an Australian setting.

Terry O'Rourke was a reckless, lovable, contradictory Irishman out of the pages of fiction. His escapades were the talk of the Monaro at the time and he has now become a sort of legend. In the bush pubs and around the camp fires in the mountains they will talk for years to come about the 'Wild Irishman', now with his ancestors, the ancient kings of Ireland.

I kept on writing away in my spare time and formed long-standing associations with the *Sydney Mail* and *Country Life*, two popular weekly publications of the day. The editor of *Country Life*, D.H. (Dave) Souter took me under his wing and taught me many things about the craft. Dave was a marvellous writer-artist whose drawings of black cats were fashionable at the time. He once won a national competition for an Australian nursery rhyme with this gem:

The Man from Menindie was counting sheep
He counted so hard that he went to sleep
    He counted by threes,

And he counted by twos,
The rams and the lambs
And the wethers and ewes.
He counted six thousand three hundred and ten
And when he woke up he'd to count them again.

I doubt if there has been a better nursery rhyme written since; it almost sends you to sleep.

After the financial collapse of O'Rourke, Mant & Co, I drifted back to Sydney and one hot summer's day in 1925, on impulse, I walked into the offices of the *Daily Telegraph* in Castlereagh Street and asked to see the chief of staff (the hiring and firing man). I was greatly surprised to be given an immediate interview and even more surprised to discover that the chief of staff was a gentleman named Alec H. Chisholm. He seemed a gruff sort of man but apparently a warm heart beat under his rugged exterior.

'I seem to remember your name,' he said. 'Something you wrote?'

'I wrote a book once,' I said, 'and you reviewed it. Nobody else did and nobody bought it.'

'Did I give you a good review?'

'Not really, but you said I had an underlying talent.'

'Ever done any newspaper reporting?'

'Not really.'

'It's a different ball game, sonny, but I'll test that underlying talent of yours. There must be something wrong with me today; maybe it's the heat. Come and see me at half past two next Monday afternoon.'

So began a career in journalism that has lasted for more than sixty years. It killed any pretensions I had of becoming a writer of literary consequence. Journalese, and later cablese, took over but there were compensations.

I quickly learnt many tricks of the newspaper trade and embarked on a life of fascinating and sometimes exciting close-ups of people and events. My police press pass took me behind the scenes of crime, politics, sport, the theatre, big business and the social scene. I loved every moment of it and became pretty good at it. I had found at last what I had been seeking in life and one day, I vowed, I would try to storm that Fleet Street again.

The time I joined the *Daily Telegraph*, soon to become the *Daily Telegraph Pictorial* and Sydney's first tabloid daily, was in the middle of the last hurrah of the so-called Roaring Twenties. It was the Jazz Age, the days of Flaming Youth, air heroes galore, Rudolph Valentino, mah jong parties, Coue-ism, Freud-ism and a world revolution in manners and morals. Girls suddenly began to wear short dresses, bob their hair, use lipstick, flatten their breasts to look boyish and smoke cigarettes in public and generally flaunt a liberation and permissiveness that would seem absurdly puritanical today. The cigarettes were ordinary cigarettes, marijuana was not known to young people then. Although alcohol flowed freely and there was a thriving sly grog trade, a 'drug scene' scarcely existed. Any drug smuggling was confined to opium to be used in sleazy dens in Sydney's Chinese quarter. They were wild, light-hearted days, reflected in the newspapers and the blithe mood of the journalists who reported it all. It was as if everybody in some mysterious way knew that the Depression was just around the corner, and that life would never be the same again.

I became friendly with Hugh Buggy, a crime and sports writer on the *Sun*, known as the Damon Runyon of Sydney. Everybody loved Hughie, including the criminals and madams of Sydney's many bordellos. I went on many dubious excursions with Hughie. His face and name were an open sesame to the most notorious houses of ill fame and sly grog joints in the 'dirty half-mile' of Kings Cross. It should be emphasised that Hughie's visits to these dens of vice were strictly in pursuit of crime stories, though he was not above sharing a bottle of beer with the inmates. A brothel was about the only place beer was obtainable after licensed hours in those days. He got many a scoop that way.

If you were with Hughie on those after-dark excursions into the underworld, no harm would come to you. The protection was certainly needed. Those were the days of the Darlinghurst razor gangs, when vicious thugs roamed the streets with safety razor blades embedded in pieces of cork. The face slashings, especially of prostitutes, were horrific, to be gaudily embellished by Hugh Buggy's purple prose.

You did not have to understand what Hugh was saying to like him—in fact, very few people understood what he was saying half the time. But a kind of Esperanto broke through his quick-fire mumbles and you could pick up a word here and there. His long-time copy-taker at the *Sun* was Owen Hoy, the reason being that he was the only person on the paper who could interpret Hugh. They were a great team, and great drinking mates after hours. If you were with them on those occasions you could always ask Owen, 'What did he say?' if you were in real doubt. The story goes that Hugh once telephoned a big-shot bureaucrat in Melbourne for a story and mumbled, 'Buggy here'. 'And bugger you, too!' the angry bureaucrat is supposed to have replied.

Hugh also reported wrestling and cricket, his writing style consisting of an absolute avalanche of alliterate adjectives. I have mentioned Hugh Buggy in some detail because he reported the bodyline tour for the *Sun* and it is generally conceded that he coined the word 'bodyline', though there were other claimants.

I went through the journalistic mill from menial tasks and small-time reporting to more important work. I got up at 4 a.m. to catch a Stannard's launch to meet arriving overseas liners and cargo vessels in mid-stream to get stories for shipping rounds. I became a member of the New South Wales parliamentary press gallery in the days of Jack Lang, the Big Fella, sitting next to that wayward comic genius,

Lennie Lower, of the *Daily Guardian*. I covered the aerial arrivals and departures of Charles Kingsford Smith and John Ulm in their record-breaking *Southern Cross*. Smithy became an everlasting hero to me, with his infectious grin and easy-going manner. His eyes had greatness in them. I accompanied our police roundsman on a couple of murder cases but police work did not appeal to me. I even had a stint with the girls of our social department, covering the annual polo matches in Sydney and the 'social' doings of the country set.

The assignment I liked most was a weekly review of the Tivoli Theatre's change of vaudeville program, although you could scarcely have regarded me as a dramatic critic. The Tiv was in Castlereagh Street, not far from the National where Stiffy and Mo reigned supreme. When vaudeville died, it became the Mayfair cinema and is now a supermarket.

The Tivoli's press agent was young Bill Maloney and we became friends. I got to meet many of the old greats of vaudeville, although most of them came to Australia well past their prime. There was Jack Benny, Gracie Fields, the Kellaways, Fred, Gus and Kitty Bluett, Harry Lauder, Little Tich, Ella Shields, George Wallace and many others. I remember how Bill Maloney and I were once invited to visit the Ingenues, an orchestra of twenty-two American college girls, in their block of flats in East Sydney. The girls were very talented and attractive. We set off in high hopes of an evening of debauchery but alas, the ingenues all turned out to be lesbians.

My big journalistic chance for my first by-line came on 3 November 1927. (In those days, by-lines in newspapers were hard to come by and were greatly cherished. It was the ultimate accolade for a young reporter. By-lines today have no value or prestige. Every reporter seems to write under one. This is a dangerous practice as the writer's personal views can intrude into hard news and perhaps be slanted.)

On the afternoon of 3 November 1927, more than forty

people died when the ocean liner *Tahiti* ran down and sank the Sydney Harbour ferryboat *Greycliffe*. The dead included many children returning from school to their homes in the eastern suburbs. Pitiful scenes were witnessed as relatives waited anxiously for news of survivors on a Circular Quay wharf near the Coroner's Court in George Street and the Taronga Park Zoo wharf at Bradleys Head.

I was summoned to the office of the *Telegraph*'s editor, George Cockerill, a veteran Melbourne journalist. 'Sit down, Gilbert,' he said. 'I am going to offer you a big chance. I want you to go down to the Quay and write a heart-rending story of the people waiting down there. The scenes will probably be very distressful to you, but I want you to put your heart and soul into it and make the reader feel the agonies of the mothers and wives waiting for news of their loved ones. I remember once as a young reporter being sent to cover a mine disaster in Victoria. I wrote how the women sat weeping and wringing their hands at the pithead as the bodies were brought to the surface. I described how some of the women were knitting stoically like Madame Defarge as she watched the aristocrats being taken to the guillotine in the French Revolution. That story made my name. . . '

I wasn't too clear about the analogy of Madame Defarge with a mine disaster but dutifully made my way to the wharf where the bodies were being recovered. Mr Cockerill was right. The scenes were distressing in the extreme and genuinely affected me. But today, when I re-read the story I wrote, I am slightly sickened. It was unadulterated tear-jerking in the worst possible taste and, I am inclined to believe, very inventive in parts. But I had no intention of letting the chance go by. The story made the front page, illustrated with a drawing of a crucifix and a wreath on the waters of Sydney Harbour by our gifted cartoonist, Hal Gye.

I was summoned again to the editorial presence and Mr Cockerill was effusive in his praise of my efforts. 'I particularly liked your reference to Madame Defarge knitting as the tumbrels rolled past,' he said. 'I am going to recommend that you move up a grade.'

I do not know whether my *Greycliffe* story had anything to do with it, but Mr Cockerill's reign as editor of the *Daily Telegraph* lasted less than two years and he returned to Melbourne to become a leader writer on the *Herald*.

One night about the end of 1929 I was sitting in the reporters' room preparing to go home after my night shift when 'Blue' Greatorex, the police roundsman, burst into the room. 'There's a fire at the Ambassadors,' he cried. 'Like to come along?'

The Ambassadors was Sydney's most fashionable nightclub and the fire had got a good hold by the time we arrived. The diners and dancers had been evacuated from the building, most of them in evening dress. They were milling around outside in the street with crowds of sightseers. For some time it was a scene of considerable confusion, with shouts and screams, until the fireman got the blaze under control. Then the crowd gradually dispersed. The police and firemen packed up their gear and left the scene.

The Ambassadors must have been the first of Sydney's exclusive and slightly daring nightclubs. It was a haunt of the bright young things (and the bright old things). The head waiter was an Italian named A.O. Romano and he brought a new Rudolph Valentino dimension and sophistication to Sydney's night life and eating habits. Romano was later to establish one of Sydney's most elegant restaurants bearing his name and to own the great racehorse, Bernborough. The young social lions and lionesses, the rich, the snobs, the demimonde, stars of stage and sport, all patronised the Ambassadors.

I suppose that some time during the night in question Blue must have gone back to the Golden Ball to file a story about the fire. But the next thing I remember is Blue and me sitting in an office drinking champagne with the proprietor of the Ambassadors, one of the Stewart Dawsons, I can't remember which one. Stewart Dawson was still in a state of semi-shock. He sat hunched up in a chair in his shirt sleeves, gazing out at the ruins of his nightclub. He had apparently decided to drown his sorrows in champagne and invited us to share his misery.

It was now long after midnight and the place was uncannily silent. The police and firemen had gone but there were still a few wisps of smoke floating around and an acrid smell in the air. It was a scene of utter desolation. For some reason or other, the lights were still full on and that made it look starker.

The firemen had done a thorough job with their hoses. There was at least ten centimetres of water lying on the sunken dance floor. I watched a slice of sodden bread sink slowly to the floor near the dance band podium. Nearby, a group of prawn shells floated aimlessly to and fro, looking like a toy flotilla of pink canoes. At least somebody had managed to get their prawn cocktail before the fire broke out.

We had just opened our third bottle of champagne when the silence was broken by the unexpected appearance of a lone uniformed fireman with a pair of gumboots reaching to his knees. The bright lights appeared to focus on him as he made his entrance. He was a middle-aged man with a pointed beard and he seemed to have a definite mission as he sloshed into the water on the dance floor. I was sorry to see the small wave he created sink the prawn shells. The fireman seemed unaware of our presence and we watched, with a sort of mesmerised fascination, his subsequent actions.

Having reached the centre of the dance floor he proceeded, slowly and deliberately, to undo the buttons of his fly. Then he began to relieve himself, the small splashing adding a new sound to the scene. 'I've always wanted to piddle on the dance floor of the Ambassadors,' he said aloud.

It was not conceivable that one fireman had returned to the scene simply to relieve himself on the dance floor. There had to be some deeper significance in the ritual he was performing and I thought I knew what had brought him back.

My intuition told me that he was piddling on all he thought the Ambassadors stood for—the idle rich, the spongers and hangers-on, the exhibitionists, the shams, hyprocrises and inequalities of a social system he despised yet envied. He was relieving a long-suppressed contempt for this playground of the rich, rather than his bladder, and obviously he felt better for it. He was not to know that the fire at the Ambassadors was, in fact, the funeral pyre of the Roaring Twenties, the last hurrah of an extravagant decade.

The fireman had finished and began buttoning up his fly. 'I've always wanted to piddle on the dance floor of the Ambassadors,' he repeated, glaring defiantly in our direction as he caught sight of us, 'and now I've done it.'

Stewart Dawson half rose in a surge of anger, then slumped back into his chair. 'Oh! . . . What's the use?' he said with an air of futility. 'Let's open another bottle of champagne.'

I should mention here that at the *Telegraph Pictorial* there was another link with the bodyline to come. One of the reporters on the staff was Jack Fingleton, destined to become a Test cricketer and to play a prominent part in the War of 1932–33. We had another big cricket connection in the person of A.G. (Johnnie) Moyes, the news editor. A noted interstate cricketer himself, he was largely instrumental in 'discovering' Don Bradman at Bowral and taking him to Sydney. Johnnie became a star radio cricket commentator and wrote many books on the game.

I was playing quite a bit of cricket myself at this stage with a city press team we had formed and I loved the game.

I recall one rather shameful occasion when we played a

game against a team from Picton, some fifty miles west of Sydney. The game took place on a paddock at Bargo, some miles further west and most of us got lost trying to find the place. Moreover, we had dawdled on our way from Sydney in our cars, with comfort stops at various hostelries en route. I had Tom Goodman, of the *Sydney Morning Herald*, in my 1926 Morris Cowley and we stayed overlong at the St Marys pub with Ted Long, veteran wicketkeeper with the World War I AIF team. Eventually we all assembled at Bargo a couple of hours late to find to our horror an angry mayor of Picton and a large crowd of spectators. Cricket-conscious Bargo was near Bradman country at Bowral and they had all come to see Fingo, then on the verge of Test selection. Fingo obliged with a slashing 50 or so, the mayor of Picton accepted our apologies, the kegs were broached and a good time was had by one and all. Cricket is a great leveller.

After about four years on the *Telegraph*, I reckoned I had enough experience and money to have another shot at Fleet Street. I was given a farewell party by fellow journalist, Stan East, and his wife, Milba, at their Bondi cottage. It lasted for three days and three nights, the guests coming and going in relays. Among them was Lennie Lower and Sydney's undisputed Queen of Bohemia, Dulcie Deamer, and a host of journalists, actors, musicians and other creatures of the night.

After the second day and night, the neighbours complained to the police. Such was the charisma of Stanley East that the neighbours and the police succumbed to the 'if you can't beat 'em, join 'em' syndrome. At one stage I could have sworn I saw the figures of the postman and one of our garbage collectors swaying through the fog of tobacco smoke and alcohol fumes. Anything was an excuse for the East parties and I believe Lennie Lower based many of the hilarious scenes in his classic comedy, *Here's Luck*, on them.

Early in 1930 I was poured into the liner *Esperance Bay*

at Walsh Bay, accompanied by a string of lurching carriers with my luggage, a scene reminiscent of an African safari. I regained consciousness about two days later as we entered Hobart harbour.

3

Ye Olde Leather Bottle

It was not the best of times to seek one's fortune in Fleet Street as the Great Depression was beginning to bite. I was lucky to have an introduction from Stan East to Denis Gulliver, a freelance New Zealander who had been living at Edgware in north London for some years. He was older than I was but we clicked at once and he invited me to live in his house rent-free. Denis lived there alone as he was divorced from his wife. Some funny things were to happen at Wairoa, as his house was named.

Denis was making a comfortable living writing 'one-liners' of seldom more than twenty words each, chiefly for the famous Charivari page of *Punch* magazine. He sent them out in batches of twenty or more to various other London newspapers and magazines, submitting the rejections to other publications until all were sold. They were worth only up to five shillings each (double that from *Punch*) but Denis's many acceptances amounted to a tidy amount each week.

Denis sportingly taught me the tricks of the one-liner trade and allowed me to compete with him until I found a job. Here are some of my published efforts (they may seem infantile but they kept the wolf from the Wairoa door.).

'Artist's insolvency.' Sounds as if he had been overdrawing.
A film is to be made of a baby's first year. It should be a scream.
'Mussolini author of a play.' No doubt he dictated it.
The Eastern fruit market is increasing despite old-fashioned methods, we read. Out of date plants, in fact.

'Post Office Girl's Romance,' says a headline. Caught the male in time.

The trick, of course, was to make up the joke, then manufacture a headline for it.

Life at Edgware reminded me somewhat of the Gudgeon family in Lennie Lower's *Here's Luck*. Denis was the subject of a never-ending crusade for higher alimony by his ex-wife. She made periodic visits to the cottage at Edgware to demand more money and they were noisy and frightening affrays.

By some means Denis seemed to receive advance warning of these impending visits. We locked all windows and doors and hid under the sofa or in cupboards when this stout and angry-looking woman hove in sight. There would ensure great banging on doors and windows as we cringed in our hiding-places. Eventually the ex-Mrs Gulliver would retreat, sometimes treading on a few flower beds in the front garden to show her displeasure.

Often, after a visit of this sort and when the all-clear had sounded, we sought solace at an old pub named Ye Olde Leather Bottle about half a mile away. These were the days (and they may be the same now) when there was great class distinction in English pubs and inns. There was often a saloon bar and a public bar facing each other with a counter and glass barrier down the middle. Drinkers could see each other across the dividing glass but their station in life remained separated. The saloon bar was strictly for collar-and-tie men, while the public bar was reserved for the labouring class.

I remember once seeing a huge navvy in bowyangs and working boots enter the saloon bar and ask for a pint of ale. The publican looked him over critically and gestured to the public bar. 'The other side,' he said and the navvy meekly and apologetically moved across to his proper station in life. I wondered what would have happened in an

Australian pub where the only distinction between a saloon and a public bar was the price.

Denis and I frequented the public bar at Ye Olde Leather Bottle, though at first the regulars seemed to feel that we were out of bounds. But then, as we showed no signs of 'slumming' condescension, we were accepted. When it was discovered that I was an Australian and Denis was a New Zealander, it seemed to explain everything. We were regarded as eccentrics and if there is anyone the English warm to it is an eccentric. We joined them in songs and 'shouted' drinks for the mob.

And there was the Blue Po, which became a symbol for everything and was known throughout Edgware. The Blue Po was an old-fashioned blue chamber pot which we carried with us to the pub. When we had all the bitter ale we could drink, we asked the publican to 'fill her up' and we would stagger somewhat unsteadily back to Wairoa with the Blue Po filled to the brim and slopping all over the place. Sometimes we would invite our next-door neighbour, a mad old inventor named Uncle, to join us. Uncle was always going to make his fortune with an invention but he never did.

In addition to my fatuous one-liner jokes, I also started to round up candidates for a series of interviews with British literary figures by arrangement with the *Sydney Mail* magazine in Sydney. Some of them are little known today but they were big literary fish in the 1930s. Kipling, Shaw and Galsworthy eluded me but were gracious enough to answer my letters. They included Noel Coward, A.A. (Winnie the Pooh) Milne, Hugh Walpole, Rose Macauley, Ian Hay and Colonel H.C. McNeile (he wrote under the name of 'Sapper' and created Bulldog Drummond, a sort of James Bond of the day).

The Milne interviews resulted in a scoop of sorts. During it, he told me that he was not going to write any more

Christopher Robin poems. 'They were written for him when he was very young,' he said, 'and now he is nearly ten. They were sort of inspirations from Christopher Robin himself and somehow I think one could not recapture the whimsical spirit of those days.'

With Milne's permission, I submitted the story to the London *Daily Herald*, which published it as 'Christopher Robin is dead—killed by growing up'. They paid me twenty-five guineas for it. Twenty-five guineas!—there was great celebration at Wairoa that night and an excursion to Ye Olde Leather Bottle, with the Blue Po and Uncle, the mad inventor.

Then, out of the blue, I landed a temporary job with the Australian Newspapers Cable Service (ANCS) in London. This was a news-gathering cooperative transmitting British and overseas news of Australian interest to Australia. The head man at the time was Thomas Dunbabin, a noted Australian editor and former Rhodes Scholar. This was real money at last and the Blue Po made its way to Ye Olde Leather Bottle again and the regulars rejoiced with me.

The nerve-centre of my ANCS 'round' was Australia House in the Strand, presided over by the Australian High Commissioner in London, Sir Granville Ryrie. By a stroke of good luck, I already knew Sir Granville as his two daughters, 'Dee' and 'Da', were members of our young group during my Cooma days. Sir Granville was a blunt and likeable soldier–politician–grazier, whose family were pioneers at Michelago on the Monaro. 'Bull' Ryrie fought with distinction as a tough and popular Australian Light Horse leader in the Boer War and World War I.

All Australians overseas congregated at Australia House, not only for passports and other official needs, but to browse over the newspapers and magazines in the library for news of home.

I paid regular calls on Sir Granville and other section heads for news items. And it was there that I made a crucial contact that took me a giant step along the road to bodyline.

Herbie Smith worked for the immigration section and had been captain of the Australia House cricket team for a number of years. Although he was over fifty, he was still a very capable bowler and batsman. Australia House competed in the London Club Cricket Conference, an organisation consisting of dozens of cricket clubs sponsored by banks, insurance offices, business houses and other cricket-loving bodies. The standard of play was sufficiently high to gain the LCCC representative matches against visiting overseas teams as a lead up to Test matches.

On one visit to Herbie he happened to mention that his team was a man short for a match against Barclays Bank at Rickmansworth, north of London, on the following Sunday. With the colossal cheek of the young, I immediately volunteered to fill the vacancy, boasting of my imaginary prowess with bat and ball. I set out in a Greenline coach for Rickmansworth on the Sunday a mass of nerves and sense of impending doom. To my enormous surprise, I performed quite well, taking two difficult catches and scoring 15 runs not out. A latent talent, hitherto unknown, had emerged and cricket, playing and watching, was to become a passion with me for the rest of my life.

I became a regular member of the Australia House team but only just. I was usually the eleventh man and sometimes did not get a bat, but I did not care. Just being on a cricket field in cream flannels was magic to me.

1930 was the Year of the Bradman in England. The Boy from Bowral was on his way to making more records than a gramophone company, as one wit put it. He was to score 236 runs in his first match in England, the first of three successive double centuries, and became the first visiting batsman to score 1,000 runs before the end of May. He went on to blaze a Test record score of 334, 309 of which came on the first day, 105 before lunch, 115 in the afternoon and 89 after tea. During the tour he made 2,960 runs, averaging 98.66. In Test matches he made four centuries and 974 runs, averaging 139.14.

At the end of the tour a lot of English cricketers were wondering how on earth to contain Don Bradman when England would tour Australia two years hence, in 1932–33. One of them was a dour Anglo-Scot named Douglas Robert Jardine.

No wonder Don Bradman was big news on that first trip of his to England. The public in Australia and England could not get enough about him on and off the field. And that was why Mr Dunbabin called me into his office one morning.

'Do you know anything about cricket?'

'Why, yes,' I replied. 'As a matter of fact I'm a regular member of the Australia House team.'

Mr Dunbabin explained that a request had come from the Sydney *Daily Guardian* for special coverage of the Australian tour to supplement their service from Reuters and Geoffrey Tebbutt of the Australian Press Association. The *Guardian* had been founded by Robert Clyde Packer, Kerry's grandfather, in 1923. Did I think I could do the job? Too right I could or words to that effect.

'Well,' said Mr Dunbabin, 'pack your bags and get up to Nottingham for the First Test as soon as you can.'

(Bless you Herbie Smith! I said to myself as I hurried out of the room, and thank heavens, Mr Dunbabin, you didn't ask me whether I had ever reported cricket before.)

As it happened, the *Guardian* job was a pushover. What they required were merely stories about the game and the Test match atmosphere, and I had the experience to give them what they wanted. I did not have to worry about the scores or the technicalities. I've kept the *Guardian* newspaper cuttings over the years and I must say it's pretty dull reading today. I was no Neville Cardus, that's for sure. Take this piece about the Fifth Test at The Oval in London:

ALL ENGLAND IS AT FEVER HEAT

From our Special Representative with the team
London, Thursday.

All England is excited over the deciding Test match, which commences at the Oval on Saturday. Some idea of the interest being taken in the game can be gauged from the fact that one man hired a window of a house near the Oval to watch the Australians practice today.

Victor Richardson's batting was a feature of the practice. He was so light-hearted about it all that he practised in a bowler hat, much to the delight of the crowd which gathered to look on.

Two private stands are being erected at the Oval to seat more spectators. The 30,000 main seats have been sold out for some days.

These private seats will be sold at eight shillings and sixpence daily. And an old house was demolished to provide the extra accommodation.

Windows overlooking the Oval have been sold at a price of six shillings per day for the duration of the Test.

One landlady has provided accommodation for 40 persons in a big room with three windows. She hopes to clear £150 during the Test by charging each person two shillings and sixpence a day.

Nearly 2,000 persons, it is expected, will view the Test in this way.

More significant was another rather heady dispatch of mine about play in Australia's second innings in the Test:

LARWOOD IN ROLE
OF 'KILLER'

From our special representative
London, Wednesday

This Bradman is lion-hearted, physically and figuratively.

He made a double century despite the whirlwind rib-breaking tactics of Larwood.

Don was doubled up with pain when a terrifically fast ball struck him in the chest. Shortly afterwards another Larwood ball crashed on to his fingers.

It would be hard to realise the pain he was suffering as he flogged the bowling. When Jackson shook him by the hand after his double century Don winced in agony.

It was real cricket courage. Larwood was in his most dangerous mood reminiscent of his Australian visit. Balls jumped from the pitch at high speed and it seemed as if Bradman and Jackson would be seriously injured.

Jackson threw up his head in pain when a Larwood ball struck his chest. He afterwards seemed to be sick, frequently leaning on his bat.

Later, a ball from Hammond cracked him on the elbow. They were anxious moments for Australia as the balls hurtled towards the batsmen's heads.

I wince with pain myself when I re-read the heading. As I was to find out later on, anyone less like a killer than Harold Larwood would be hard to imagine.

The significance of the report was that in later years it would be claimed that Bradman's 'uncomfortable' attitude towards bumpers during that innings led to the first hatching of a plot for a bodyline attack in Australia two years later.

I became more enslaved than ever by cricket during these experiences on the highest level. I marvelled at the batsmanship of the young lions of the Australian team, Don Bradman, Archie Jackson and Stan McCabe. I waxed lyrical over them in my reports to the *Guardian*. I did not meet Don Bradman personally during these Tests, though I once went up in the same lift with him at the team's hotel. I could now boast: 'I went up in a lift with Don Bradman!'

I pretended to emulate some of the Test skills I had witnessed when I returned to the Australia House matches. The cricket we played was not village cricket, with the vicar and the blacksmith cavorting about, and it was not Test cricket. But it was serious enough to have real umpires in white coats and there was no skylarking. The Australia House side was formidable on occasions, as we could draw on the services of Australian doctors, lawyers and others doing postgraduate courses at English universities. On one occasion three of us had to stand down to make way for a trio of current Sheffield Shield players. They included Brian (afterwards Sir Brian) Hone, of South Australia, later a distinguished headmaster.

The charm of cricket is that it is a team game and also an individual game. It is also an exacting and unforgiving game. In golf, for instance, if you make a bad shot, you can recover with some good shots. In cricket, you have only one chance. If you drop a catch, you have to live with the shame of it. If you are bowled or caught or out by some other ways as a batsman, you are finished for the day.

And yet it has an enchantment all of its own. It was bliss to be fielding in the deep in the long English summer twilights, with a fierce commitment to defend one's own territory and to send the ball whizzing towards the wicketkeeper. Sheer exhilaration to get on to a ball in the middle of the bat and drive it racing to the boundary, to the applause of 'Well played, sir!' from somebody among the onlookers. Yes, they were the days when 'it isn't cricket' really meant something far beyond the game itself. We played for the sheer love of the game and never thought about it being commercialised by the entrepreneurs and the players put into fancy dress.

We played on some beautiful grounds inside and outside London owned by banks and other institutions. When the match was over we would adjourn to the dressing room or the local pub to play the game all over again, downing pints of bitter ale and telling cricket stories, which are inexhaustible. And to pray for a fine day next Sunday when we were down to play against the Prudential Insurance Company at their ground in Berkshire.

Although it was the Year of the Bradman, another Australian sportsman was hitting the headlines at the same time. Walter Lindrum, master of the billiards cue, was such a freakish player that they had to change the rules of the game to check his phenomenal scoring and give the other fellows a chance. He made a world record break of 4,137 in 2 hours 55 minutes in London in 1932 which still stands.

The mastery of their respective games earned Bradman the title of the Lindrum of Cricket, while Lindrum became known as the Bradman of Billiards. Both were short in stature but strongly built. Both were quiet, modest, undemonstrative men. Lindrum was ten years older than Bradman. He is said to have given Bradman a number of lessons in billiards but there is no record of Lindrum taking cricket lessons from the Don.

I got to know Walter Lindrum very well and sent many stories about him back to Australia while working for ANCS. It was quite an experience watching him compiling breaks in his smooth, effortless style, at Thurston's, the holy of holies and Lord's of billiards (in Piccadilly, I think). The Lindrum ascendency had given billiards a new glamour and popularity. Fashionable men and women attended the night sessions in evening dress. Lindrum played before royalty and the aristocracy and ordinary devotees of the green cloth.

The hushed atmosphere at Thurston's was that of a darkened pagan amphitheatre, the congregation worshipping the vivid green baize tablecloth in the centre, fiercely illuminated by electric light. The only sounds were the click of the billiards balls, one red, two white, as Lindrum made them do his bidding, caressing them gently around the table cushions for his extraordinary nursery cannons.

During his career, Walter Lindrum established 57 world records and made more than 800 breaks of 1,000 or more. In 1930 he conceded 7,000 points to several of his main rivals and still won. He died in 1960, aged sixty-two. His grave in the Melbourne General Cemetery was decorated with a marble-topped billiards table, complete with a cue and three brass billiards balls. The irony is that Lindrum's rare skill helped to kill the game in favour of pool, or snooker.

My job with the ANCS went on into the summer of 1931 and I had a horrible feeling that it could not last—and it didn't. The Depression deepened all over the world and one day the ANCS declared me redundant. Mr Dunbabin said he was sorry and that I had done a good job for them. If anything turned up, he would let me know.

I sat down in the cottage at Edgware again to try to make a crust as a freelance journalist, but it was a losing battle from the start. Nobody wanted one-liners any more and journalists were being retrenched in all directions. Even Denis was losing much of his one-liner market. I was not able to contribute enough towards my board and lodging and felt I could not sponge on Denis any longer. I did not have enough money for a ship fare back to Australia and was too ashamed to send brother John another 'Broke Gilbert' cable.

So I went to Herbie Smith at Australia House for help and good old Herbie did not let me down. He saw to it that I jumped the queue as welfare officer to the last shipload of British migrants going to Australia. Ironically, the ANCS reported it back to Australia as follows:

The *Jervis Bay* will leave for Australia next month with the last group of boy migrants, ten of whom are going to Queensland and the last welfare officer—Mr Gilbert Mant, a Sydney journalist. A waiting list of 27 would-be welfare officers included three clergymen.

(Some time later I received a letter from Jack Quayle, resident cartoonist of the Sydney *Daily Telegraph Pictorial*: 'The story that you were returning as WELFARE officer to some Pommy lads was a standing joke in the office for weeks. You can imagine the material it gave Chis to display his brilliant wit. You couldn't do worse by returning here at the present time. Depression is not the name for it—Lang has taxed us five per cent on our salaries and now the Associated Newspapers wants to deduct another 15 per cent. Bright outlook isn't it?')

So there it was. Sorrowfully I packed my bags. I had gone off to England in high hopes and now I was returning with my tail between my legs, a failure for the second time. What would I do when I got back? Go back to Cooma and trap rabbits? From what I could hear, things in journalism were parlous. No chance of a job there, either. I'd be worse off than the boy migrants whose welfare I was supposed to be preserving.

4

The House of Reuter

The telephone rang. It was Mr Dunbabin. 'I'm ringing you, Gilbert, to tell you that Reuters are looking for staff. They are undergoing a big reorganisation and need a few experienced journalists. It's worth a try. It would help you if you had an influential backer of some sort. Have you got one?'

I certainly had. I had Uncle Reg, my father's brother. Reginald Mant had been born at Gigoomgan Station in Queensland. After a brilliant school and university career, he entered the Indian Civil Service and worked his way to the top as a sort of financial genius. Sir Reginald Mant, KCSI, KCIE, was now a member of the Council for India and an influential man.

The Council for India of fifteen members was established by the British government in 1858 after the East India Company was deprived of its governing powers over India. The council acted as an advisory body to the Secretary of State for India, responsible to parliament. It was disbanded in 1937 as India moved towards self-government and partition into India and Pakistan. Uncle Reg had a massive office in the India Office. From its wide windows we used to have close-ups of King George V and members of the royal family during official occasions in Whitehall.

(I have a large photograph of the wedding reception given by Reginald and Eileen [née Tandy] Mant at Simla in 1905. They were married by the Bishop of Lahore and the 200 guests represented the cream of the Raj Establishment of the day in India. Lords and ladies and a countess or two in abundance and names such as Birdwood, Kitchener, Carberry, Tandy, Poynter, Sheepshanks, Wilberforce, Balfour, Cumberlege, Shekelton, Beresford Lovett and DeCourcy Hamilton. The group photograph was taken outdoors with a huge carpet on the ground and a background of lush and exotic Indian trees and vines. The wide floral hats of the ladies were a sight to behold, and their dainty parasols. Looking at it today, I am surprised and somewhat chagrined to note that there is not one maharajah or Indian of any kind among the guests. This was not the case some twenty-five years later when I was invited to dinner parties by Uncle Reg and Aunt Eileen at 54 Onslow Square, South Kensington. They were fascinating affairs where one was likely to meet Indian princes, British generals, politicians (even a Cabinet minister sometimes) and once Harry Oppenheimer, the South African mining magnate, head of De Beers diamond monopoly. I learnt to pass the port the right way and my education grew apace.)

I was bolstered that I could perhaps also call on Sir Granville Ryrie as a referee but it was not necessary. Uncle Sir Reg's name was a golden password to Reuters; his name was in the news regularly as India became restive for independence. I was asked to present myself forthwith for an interview with Mr Bernard Rickatson-Hatt, editor-in-chief, at the Reuter building at Blackfriars, overlooking the Thames.

Like a good journalist I did my homework and read everything I could find on Reuters. On the day of the interview, the neighbours saw to it that I had on my best suit and that my necktie was straight (I had a nervous habit of fiddling with it). I cleaned my teeth twice and took the underground train at Edgware for London.

Mr Rickatson-Hatt did not look at all like a newspaper executive, or even a newspaperman. He was fortyish, balding, impeccably dressed, with a bristling moustache and a quick clipped English accent. He looked exactly like an ex-Guards officer which indeed he was. I couldn't guess how or why he had taken up journalism, but he had a crusading enthusiasm for the job of getting Reuters out of its rut and bringing it up to date. I could tell that the place needed a shake-up. The building itself looked moribund, the office furniture and equipment and some of the staff looked in need of rejuvenation. It had a depressing feel about it.

Mr Rickatson-Hatt asked me a lot of questions about myself and tested my knowledge of current affairs. Did I think that Britain would soon go off the gold standard? To which I replied non-committally, not having the vaguest idea about it. At some stage I modestly mentioned that I played cricket with Australia House but he did not seem particularly interested. He did not forget it, though.

The upshot was that he offered me an indeterminate trial period. Four weeks and the *Jervis Bay* was to sail. I would have to go on with my welfare officer job or take a chance with Reuters. I chose the chance. If I failed in my trial, well it would be the poorhouse, if such things still existed.

I had not worked there very long before I realised what Mr Rickatson-Hatt had meant and why he wanted to change these things, even to the extent of employing an Australian. I also knew that I would have little difficulty in holding my position there with my Australian training, though I would have to rethink my journalism to conform with the Reuter twin doctrines—Objectivity and Accuracy.

Reuters worldwide reputation was still intact but it had not moved with the times in the gathering and dissemination of news. Cable and wireless were now carrying news almost instantaneously but there seemed to be no real sense of urgency in the Reuter office in 1931. It still dealt in long-winded hand-outs and lengthy official statements from Downing Street, paying little attention to the needs of the tabloid newspapers and upcoming entrepreneurial newspaper barons. Shorter, brighter stories were required as well as the sterner stuff that had made the name of Reuter a bible of authenticity.

The place on the Thames certainly had an old-fashioned air about it with some of the younger staff completely devoid of 'news sense' or any inkling of the needs of a modern newspaper. They had none of the basic training of an Australian journalist, apparently taking up journalism as 'jolly good fun'. One young man was the son of an Irish peer who was actually paying Reuters a hefty premium for allowing him to work there. He was an awfully nice chap but quite hopeless at his work and had no-one to teach him it.

On the other hand, the young fellow at the desk adjoining me had plenty of go in him and a lively sense of imagination. He was a twenty-three-year-old Old Etonian named Ian Fleming. He had been with Reuters for two years, cooking up James Bond, no doubt. His older brother, Peter Fleming, was already an accomplished author and traveller.

I had to learn to be scrupulously accurate and careful. At Reuters, your story went all over the world, where somewhere, at any time of the day or night, a newspaper was being put to bed. A single mistake in a name or a date or a place would have to be corrected all over the world at financial cost and loss of prestige. The Reuter accuracy was to become a fetish to me for the rest of my journalistic life, much to the annoyance of colleagues and others.

I should say here that I got to like BR-H and I think he regarded me as his protégé despite being a colonial. I also learnt that he possessed one of the most extensive libraries of erotica in London but I didn't know what that had to do with it. I was with him in his crusade to take Reuters out of its carrier-pigeon mentality and compete on fairer terms with the other world agencies.

Reuters (pronounced Royters or just Royter) was born

when a young German bank clerk named Julius de Reuter threw some pigeons into the air from his tiny office in Aix-la-Chapelle in 1849. Around the neck of each pigeon was attached a silken bag and inside the bags were the latest prices of bonds, stocks and shares from the local bourse written on thin sheets of tissue paper. The pigeons flew swiftly to their dovecotes at Brussels and subscribers received the market information some hours ahead of the horse-drawn mail coaches.

When the first cable was laid under the English Channel between Calais and Dover, Reuter transferred himself to London. At first, he confined himself to stock exchange information, but soon enlarged his business to cover first commercial news and then general news. From those humble beginnings grew the world's greatest news-gathering organisation.

Mr Reuter, who became a British citizen, had imagination, daring and skill. There was no trans-Atlantic cable when the American Civil War broke out in 1861. News from America went by mail steamer and was telegraphed to Reuters in London from Riches Point, County Cork, in Ireland. One day Reuter discovered that a rival agency had entered the field of American news. Dealing with the threat with characteristic ingenuity, he acquired a small steamer and instructed his agent in New York to enclose his war dispatches in an hermetically sealed tin box with a distinctive flag attached to it. Somewhere off the coast of Ireland the purser of the incoming American mail steamer threw the box overboard. The Reuter steamer found the box by its flag and rushed the special dispatches to Crookhaven where the ingenious Mr Reuter had erected a private telegraph line to London. His competitors were beaten by eight hours.

This method gained Reuter one of the most famous scoops in newspaper history. When President Abraham Lincoln was assassinated in 1865, the Reuter agent in New York found to his chagrin that the mail boat to Ireland had just sailed. He hired a tug and chased the steamer out to sea, just managing to heave on board the tin box containing the news of Lincoln's death. Thanks to his enterprise, Reuter had the news of the assassination a clear week ahead of everybody else. Scoops of such nature are not possible today when news, and even pictures, are flashed instantaneously over the whole face of the globe by radio, cable and satellite.

Julius de Reuter had not been the first to exploit the agency idea. A Frenchman, Charles Havas, established a regular carrier-pigeon news service from Paris in 1835. Then Bernhard Wolff, a German, used the first telegraphic service to syndicate news from Berlin in 1849. There was fierce competition between Reuter, Havas and Wolff until 1870 when the big three signed an agreement dividing the world between them with exclusive preserves. Reuter got the lion's share of the deal.

The Reuter archives contain many other historic scoops. One of the most notable was the telegram received in London on 19 May 1900, giving the world the first news of the relief of Mafeking during the Boer War. It led to amazing scenes of rejoicing but there were some heart-burnings in the Reuter office on that eventful night. The news had been cabled back to South Africa, actually giving Lord Roberts, the British commander, first news of the relief—but no official confirmation was forthcoming for two days. Prime Minister Joseph Chamberlain, pressed in the House of Commons, had to admit that he had no information except the Reuter telegram, adding that he had every confidence in the traditional Reuter accuracy.

At last, two days later, confirmation came and the Reuter office breathed again. The reason for the scoop was that the Reuter correspondent had persuaded the Boers to let him remain on their side. The Boers knew before the British that Mafeking was relieved, because the British relieving force was very far from its base, and for a time out of telegraphic touch. The Reuter correspondent rushed the news out through the neutral Portuguese territory and got it to the Eastern Telegraph Company's cable at Lourenco Marquis, a couple of days before any one else. The fact that the whole British Empire should have celebrated Mafeking entirely on Reuters word was one of the greatest compliments the agency has ever been paid.

Julius de Reuter was made a baron by the German Duke of Saxe-Coburg-Gotha, a foreign honour recognised by the British government His son, Baron Herbert de Reuter, died in 1915 and his grandson, Baron Hubert de Reuter, the last of the Reuters, was killed in action in World War I in 1916, while serving with a Scottish regiment.

Enter Roderick Jones, son of a Cheshire hat salesman who was sent to South Africa as a teenager to fend for himself. Young Roderick became a journalist and part-time correspondent for Reuters, rising from that to be general manager of all Reuter affairs in South Africa. Ambitious young Jones hastened to London after Herbert de Reuter's death and at the age of only thirty-seven became managing director of Reuters Telegram Company. He was knighted in 1917 for propaganda services in World War I.

Sir Roderick went on to gain total control, converting the agency into private corporation at a cost of more than half a million pound sterling and became principal proprietor. In 1925 Jones sold 53 per cent of the Reuters shares to the Press Association (PA), Britain's main domestic news agency, collectively owned by the provincial press.

Reuters fell on bad times. All kinds of business manoeuvres went on behind the scenes during World War II and Sir Roderick Jones 'retired' (or was he pushed?) in 1941. In 1945 the Newspaper Proprietors Association of more than 100 British national proprietors joined the PA as equal partners and a Reuter Trust was formed. The aim was to maintain Reuters vital principles of accuracy and impartiality, irrespective of every outside consideration and influence.

Reuters became a public company in 1984 and today its news, mainly financial, is carried around the clock, not by pigeons but computers, to 148 different countries in the world. A sensational book, *The Price of Truth* by John Lawrenson and Lionel Barber (Mainstream Publishing, Edinburgh) was published in 1985, suggesting that corporate skullduggery had destroyed the Reuter Trust and turned it into a fabulous money-spinner. The authors described their story as one of 'greed and intrigue' by a handful of people, largely anonymous.

I've got ahead of myself, but never mind. When I joined Reuters in 1931 I knew nothing of these business machinations behind the shabby facade of the Reuter building in Blackfriars.

One thing was crystal clear—Sir Roderick Jones was unquestionably the boss. He was a dapper and vital little man and an autocrat. He was so short that it was said the chair he sat on behind his big desk was specially built up. On the few occasions when I was summoned into the Presence, he certainly seemed to tower over me. I have a recollection that the cuffs of his shirt sleeves crackled as he moved, as if they were starched, but I'm not sure of this. I must say that Sir Roderick treated me with courtesy and understanding on all occasions—except an occasion after I returned from the bodyline tour.

Reuters may have been going down the drain at the time but Sir Roderick seemed sincere in his belief in the Reuter ideals. I kept a copy of one of his speeches:

From the outset of his engagement and training, every Reuter representative has drilled into him that accuracy and impartiality must ever be his first consideration. The expression, nay, the most shadowy reflection of his political views is forbidden. He must restrict himself to straight news, despite mankind's growing passion for world gossip and all that heightens the tension and intoxication of life. That is the tradition upon which the name of Reuters has been established. Insistence on that tradition has never flagged.

Pretty old lofty ideal stuff, you'll say, and I wonder if today's Reuterians live by it?

Reuters, of course, operated twenty-four hours a day. News waited for no man, or woman. We worked in six-hour shifts at night. News came in without cessation as Reuters had a correspondent in every country in the world, the largest overseas staff of any news-gathering body in existence. It was our job to translate the cables into acceptable news items for distribution to newspapers throughout Britain and overseas.

This was not as easy as it sounds, for it meant learning a new language. The cost of press cables was quite steep, ranging from sixpence to two shillings a word. It is difficult to explain an equivalent for today but it was sufficiently expensive to require the strictest economy in words. So cablese was invented. This was based on the use of such words as cum, anti, pro, wards, un and wise to convert two or three words into one. For instance a message from the Reuter correspondent in Bangkok could be abbreviated into something like this:

RIVAL CAMBODIAN FACTIONS BEGUN FINAL REVIEW UNINATIONS PEACE TREATY AMID STRONG ILLFEELINGS ANTIKHMERROUGE REPATRIATION THOUSANDS REFUGEES PRIMINISTER HUN SAID TASK DIFFICULTER BECAUSE AMERICA UPLINKED CUMAUSTRALIA OBJECTIVE ESTABLISHING PROWESTERN STANCE JAPANWARDS

This would be translated into:

Bangkok, Wednesday—Rival Cambodian factions today began a final review of the United Nations sponsored peace treaty amid strong ill-feelings over the Khmer Rouge's repatriation of thousands of refugees.

The Cambodian Prime Minister, Mr Hun Sen, said that the task had been made more difficult because America had linked up with Australia with the object of establishing a pro-Western stance towards Japan. REUTER

There was a running argument with the cable companies over the legitimacy of our word concoctions and some of our submissions were rejected. As I remember it, we were restricted to twenty letters to a word. At times it was almost impossible to interpret some of the ingenious word inventions of our correspondents in their efforts to comply with the company's urge for economy in costs.

There is a legendary story of an American foreign correspondent in Shanghai who resigned after a blazing row by cabling his New York head office to 'Upstick job arsewards'.

Reuters were very cautious people. I was on trial for nearly six months before the decision was taken to admit me into their hallowed company. At last, on 9 September 1931, I signed an agreement with Reuters Limited on a thick parchment form decorated by a red embossed sixpenny duty stamp with a crown and thistle on it. It is quite preposterous to read it today with its provisos that an officer could not marry without the consent of Reuters or engage in any trading or commercial operation under pain of instant dismissal.

My salary was set at the munificent sum of £175 per annum, less than £4 a week or about a quarter of my old *Daily Telegraph Pictorial* salary. But I would have signed anything to get my Australian foot in the Reuter international door. Here are some of the many conditions in the agreement:

No officer is to divulge, either directly or indirectly, any
message or part of a message, or any transaction of which
he may have cognisance in discharge of his duties, or in
consequence of his connection with Reuter upon pain of
instant dismissal.

No officer is permitted to carry on any trading or commercial
operation, or to enter into, or join in speculation of any kind,
other than bona-fide investments, upon pain of instant
dismissal.

Punctuality is insisted upon.

Any case of misconduct, breach of trust or other offence,
considered by Reuters of sufficient gravity, on the part of
the Officer, will subject him to instant dismissal.

In the event of an Officer marrying without Reuters consent,
on what Reuters may deem insufficient means, Reuters shall
have the right to terminate his employment and service, by
giving to the Officer three months notice or three months
salary in lieu of notice.

The reference to commercial speculation was fair enough.
Julius de Reuter had started his agency by dealing in the
prices of stocks and shares, with much inside information.
I think it's called 'insider trading' today and people have
gone to gaol for it.

As 1932 was ushered in I looked forward to the end of
the bleak English winter and another season of cricket with
Australia House. By then I had been promoted to the
prestigious Dominions Desk. This was staffed by a group
of about six senior journalists and dealt with all news, both
inward and outward, relating to the British dominions and
colonies. Reuters had contracts to supply worldwide news
to clients in India, South America, South Africa and a mini-
service to a little British outpost at Lagos in West Africa.

Naturally enough, any messages to and from Australia
were passed over to me. Cable costs were so high, overseas
Reuter offices also supplied London with 'mailers', stories

of lesser importance and urgency sent by sea mail (there were no regular air services at that time). I remember one mailer in particular.

About the middle of February 1932, we received a lengthy mail story about the construction and completion of the now-famous Sydney Harbour Bridge to be officially opened by the New South Wales Labor premier, Jack Lang, on 19 March. It arrived in ample time to redirect the story to our offices in Europe, America and other parts of the world. Sydney was to advise us by cable of the opening and we would then cable a release of our other mail stories.

Sure enough, at about 3.30 am (London time) on 19 March a cable arrived from Sydney, 'Release bridge opening'. I was on night duty at the time and, priding myself on my Australian alertness, cabled a release to all the other contries which had our story. Then I had the story put on our own teleprinter circuit to all British newspapers. I was feeling very pleased with myself when, about thirty minutes later, a frantic cable from Sydney arrived, 'Cancel bridge opening story follows'.

It was too late. Somewhere in the world some newspaper had already had Mr Lang opening the bridge at his first attempt. What had happened has become Australian folklore. It was the middle of the Great Depression and Jack Lang (the 'Big Fella') was hated by the conservatives for his socialistic and anti-British views. An extreme right-wing group named the New Guard decided to make the opening of the Sydney Harbour Bridge a symbol of their opposition to the state Labor government.

In *This Fabulous Century*, (Lansdowne Press, Sydney, 1980), Peter Luck describes as the 'most famous last words in our history' those spoken by Lang before taking a pair of scissors to cut the ceremonial ribbon. '. . .in a few moments I shall complete the opening ceremony by severing the ribbon stretching across the highway,' said Lang. But before he could do so a New Guardsman named Captain Francis De Groot, dressed in Irish regimental uniform, rode up on a horse and slashed the ribbon with his sword. De Groot was arrested and a few days later fined £5 for offensive behaviour by a judge who, however, refused to declare him insane.

The Reuters man in Sydney had witnessed the ceremony from a tall city building and assumed that the cheering and hullabaloo meant that the bridge had been well and truly opened. It was some time before he could rectify his dreadful mistake and cable the sensational happenings. I was forgiven for spending money on release cables and corrections because the sword-slashing episode made the headlines, anyway. Nevertheless, it was an expensive mailer.

Allow me, please, to relate another more serious night-shift crisis I faced about a year later. The anxiety of it lingers with me still. I was on night shift again but, apart from a teleprinter operator, I was in sole charge of the main operations room for a couple of hours because of the sudden illness of other staff.

The Reuter building at Blackfriars was an eerie sort of place at night in any circumstance. This night the office was dimly lit and there was fog on the Thames that seemed to be seeping through the rather grimy windows. An occasional foghorn from a barge working its way up the river added to the eeriness. I felt very important, with the world's news in my hands, so to speak, but apprehensive that something untoward would occur. Something did.

At about 2 a.m. the teleprinter operator came to me. 'There's a French chappie from Havas in Paris on the phone. He's got a news item for you.'

Oh, my God, I thought, I hope he can speak English. He couldn't.

'Painlevé est mort,' he said.

'Parler vous Anglais?' I asked.

'Non.'

'Si-vous plaise,' I pleaded, calling on my schoolboy French. 'Si-vous plaise, chercher un homme qui parler Anglais. Je ne parler Francais.'

The message seemed to get through to him. I could imagine him shrugging his Gallic shoulders at the stupid Anglais and going away grumbling, to find someone who could oblige.

In the meantime, I was beset by anxiety. Who was Painlevé? Why was he mort? I knew that mort meant 'dead' but it might also mean something else. There might be two or three Painlevés. I had to make sure before I killed him all over the world. Time was the essence. I would be in serious trouble if the Exchange Telegraph Company or the British United Press (our main agency rivals) morted Painlevé before Reuters did. I located a *Gotha's Almanac* and I found a Painlevé, Paul Prudent. French scientist and politician, socialist premier of France in 1917 and 1925. Born etc. etc. It must be the man but I had to make absolutely certain.

It seemed ages before the call came from Paris from a Havas man who had obviously been pulled out of bed. Yes, he said rather testily, it was Paul Prudent and he was well and truly mort, dead, kaput, gone and rigor mortis. I breathed again and summoned the teleprinter operator. Over the wire went the story, 'FORMER FRENCH PREMIER DEAD'. The Exchange Telegraph and BUP must have been asleep, too. They did not mort Painlevé until an hour or so later. Thanks to the Bon Dieu, I was saved. These were the sort of things that sent agency men grey before their time.

5

The Unspeakable Jardine

I can't remember when I first began to take any interest in the forthcoming 1932–33 MCC tour of Australia and New Zealand. I did not associate myself with it in any way until I heard rumours of an internecine row going on between Reuters and the Press Association about who was to go to Australia with the English team. It will be recalled that the PA by that time had control of Reuters so one would imagine that the PA would have prevailed. But not so. Apparently, it had been a long-established custom for the PA to provide representatives for overseas sporting tours, but this time Reuters wanted their own staff man; after all it was an overseas tour and the PA consisted of provincial newspapers.

A wild, improbable thought came into my mind when I heard the rumours, so wild that I rejected it at once. Then it kept coming back again and again. What if I were to be sent to Australia as the Reuters and PA man? When I learnt that James Southerton was the PA's choice, the idea became more preposterous than ever. Southerton was one of England's most senior and eminent cricket writers (destined to become editor of *Wisden*, the cricketers' Bible). Even to compare Southerton and Mant was too silly for words. All I knew about cricket reporting was a brief spell with the 1930 Australian team and the production of 'atmosphere' stories. True, I had once gone up in the same lift as Don Bradman but I had no experience of ball-to-ball descriptions of a highly technical game.

And yet, the impossible dream kept recurring. The return of the prodigal in triumph; to travel in luxury liners to and from Australia at Reuters expense; to stay at all the best hotels in Perth, Adelaide, Melbourne, Sydney, Brisbane and Hobart; the glamour attached to being with the English Test team. The thought was intoxicating and persistent.

Then came a summons to the office of Mr Rickatson-Hatt, the editor-in-chief. 'Come in, old chap, and sit down. Are you still playing cricket with Australia House?'

'Yes,' I replied, the blood beginning to rush to my head. 'I took two catches last Saturday.'

'How would you like to go to Australia with the MCC team? Do you think you could do it?'

'Of course I could!' I said without hesitation. 'Why shouldn't I be able to do it? Being an Australian would make it all the more easy, I imagine.' (How wrong I was!)

'Well,' said BR-H, 'I can't promise you anything at this stage. I just wanted to find out whether you would be prepared to go. It's like this...'

We discussed the forthcoming tour and drafted out something about me on these lines: 'Mr Mant, who was born in Australia, is a Reuter staff member with wide journalistic experience. He is a competent cricketer who plays for Australian House in the LCCC competition. He was a Sydney *Daily Guardian* special representative with the Australian team during last year's England–Australia Test series...'

This would have fooled anyone, except me. It was true what it said, but it did not say whether I knew anything about cricket reporting. Neither did it say that the *Daily Guardian* had folded up shortly after the 1930 cricket series, though it would be unfair to attribute this to my cricket reports.

Look, it was sixty years ago and I was a young man wanting to get on in the world. Nobody asked me what I knew about cricket reporting so I did not enlighten them. Them that ask no questions isn't told no lies. I was merely a pawn in a much bigger game so I decided to make the most of it. Besides, there was no indication that the Australian tour would be other than routine, no hint of the drama to come. If I did not know much about cricket reporting, then I could soon learn. I loved and understood the game; the descriptive jargon would soon be mastered.

Reuters won the day and James Southerton was left lamenting. I packed my bags for the second return to Australia not as a welfare officer this time, but as a journalist sailing towards one of the biggest sporting and general news stories of the century.

Meantime there were discussions to be held with Vernon Morgan, who was in charge of Reuter sport, on a plan of campaign and the concoction of a cablese code to save money.

Morgan would have a detailed program of the tour and would know exactly where we were at any given time. The itinerary comprised twenty-two matches—five Tests, two against Australian XIs, ten against State teams and five minor country matches. A brief message from Wagga Wagga might read: '1500 FINE FAST ENGLAND TOSS BATTING'. This would be expanded into 'Wagga Wagga, Tuesday—The MCC team won the toss and are batting on a fast wicket in their two-day match against Wagga Wagga, a NSW country town. The weather was fine and there was an early attendance of about 1,500. REUTER.'

Most of the matches began at about 11 or 11.30 a.m. Australian time, or 1 or 1.30 a.m. London time. This meant that my first message would arrive in ample time to catch the stop-presses of the English morning newspapers. Stumps were drawn around 6 p.m. Australian time, or 8 a.m. London time, giving the evening papers a coverage of the whole day's play.

The Reuter service was to be taken by most of the newspapers in Britain, plus special services to South Africa, India, the West Indies and elsewhere. The service was to include a comprehensive description of play in all the principal matches with detailed scores and statistics. It was understood that my reports were to be strictly factual— Reuters Sydney office was there to cover developments outside the confines of the touring party, or comments by Australian newspapers or cricket specialists. The British newspapers themselves had their own commentators and also access to limited services by other news agencies. But as they were paying for it out of their own pockets, the majority depended on Reuter. I was too busy preparing for the assignment to realise the awesome responsibility I had undertaken or to worry about whether I was perpetrating a gigantic confidence trick. That came later. As I recall it, I was allocated a maximum limit of 25,000 words within which to cover the seven-plus months tour. (As it happened, it was to be closer to 100,000 words and nobody complained.)

The eve of my departure for Australia may be an opportune time to explain briefly what bodyline was all about for the benefit of those who have come in sixty years late or those to whom cricket is a mystery game.

It was all about stopping, or curbing, the phenomenal run-scoring abilities of Donald George Bradman, a twenty-four year-old Australian country-bred boy whose feats, or the means to stem them, were to lead the British Empire to the brink of destruction. As recorded in an earlier chapter, Bradman had dominated the Test series in England in 1930, apparently scoring centuries at will. The team who sailed for Australia in 1932 knew that there was no way they could regain the Ashes, the mythical symbol of cricket supremacy between England and Australia, unless Bradman could be tamed. But how?

It was years before details of the hatching of the bodyline plot were revealed and there are contradictions in the various 'inside stories' by those concerned. It is clear, however, that some English players in the fifth Test at Kennington Oval in 1930 (see Chapter 3) thought they detected that Bradman was 'uncomfortable' against Harold Larwood's fast bowling on a lifting pitch on the final day. George Hele, the Australian umpire who stood during all five tests in 1932–33, said he was satisfied that George Duckworth, the English wicketkeeper in 1930, had first thought of bodyline after noting what he thought was a chink in Bradman's armour.

It was also clear, as all participants have written books about it, that the real plot was hatched during a dinner at the Piccadilly Hotel in London after the team to go to Australia was chosen. The name of the game was 'fast leg theory', as the word bodyline had not yet been invented. Those attending the dinner were Arthur Carr, captain of Nottinghamshire, Douglas Jardine, captain of the touring team, Harold Larwood and Bill Voce, the two Nottinghamshire fast bowlers. One version says that Percy Fender, former flamboyant captain of Surrey, was also present.

Harold Larwood with Kevin Perkins gives a full account of the dinner in *The Larwood Story*, including these passages:

> Jardine asked me if I thought I could bowl on the leg stump making the ball come up into the body all the time so that Bradman had to play his shots to leg.
> 'Yes, I think that can be done,' I said.

And later on:

> We thought Don was frightened of sharp rising balls and we reasoned that if he got a lot of them over the leg stump he would be put off his game and be intimidated and eventually, having to direct his shots to the leg all the time, would give a catch to one of the onside fieldsmen.

That was the plan and Bradman was to foil them to some extent by moving to the leg, but that comes later.

It was revealed that Jardine discussed field placings with old F.R. Foster, the legendary English fast-medium left-hander who, with S.F. Barnes, routed Australia in 1911–12 by bowling leg theory to a packed leg field. Foster was later somewhat peeved to have his name associated with bodyline in this way.

Few of us knew any of these things that had happened as we set off for Australia. We were certainly completely unprepared for the overtones of drama, intrigue, stupidity, prejudice, excitement and national hysteria that lay ahead on the other side of the world.

The *Orontes*, a fine ship with two funnels, left Tilbury on 17 September 1932. (Fifty years later, an Australian television series on bodyline showed our ship leaving with two funnels but arriving in Fremantle some five weeks later with three funnels. I can't recall why, how or where we acquired the third one.)

The MCC party consisted of sixteen players (a seventeenth, Maurice Tate, was to follow in another ship), two managers and Bill Ferguson, the Australian-born official scorer and baggage master.

Manager Pelham (later Sir Pelham) Warner was a product of Rugby School and Oxford University. He became the Establishment's 'Mr Cricket' as a player, selector and administrator, an apostle of the 'it isn't cricket' barometer of sportsmanship. As a cricketer, he was precise and correct and a prolific scorer. In 1911–12 he led the MCC team to Australia and scored a century in his first match against South Australia. He was universally known as 'Plum' Warner, though I'm not sure whether this was because of the plum-in-his mouth voice. He had served as a diplomat with the British Foreign Office and was charm personified, a cultured English gentleman of the best type. Yet all the diplomacy he had acquired at the Foreign Office was not sufficient to carry him through the cricket crisis to come and he displayed fatal weaknesses.

Warner's co-manager and treasurer was Richard C.N. Palairet, another Establishment figure from Repton School and Oxford. A lanky, rather lugubrious and stiff English-man, with a droopy moustache, he improved on further acquaintance and was possessed of an impish sense of humour. He certainly knew how to look after the MCC's finances and once (at Toowoomba, Queensland) nearly caused an abandonment of the match because of an argument over a few shillings. We called him 'Dirty Dick' for no apparent reason other than it was the name of a comic strip character.

There were only three other newspaper representatives travelling with the team in the ship. Such a small press contingent was unusual but it was Great Depression times and newspaper budgets were tight. Anyhow, they knew there would always be a Reuter.

The London *Evening Standard* was represented by Bruce Harris, their lawn tennis writer. I believe his appointment ahead of their cricket writer, E.W. (Jim) Swanton, had created another sort of Southerton–Mant domestic controversy. Bruce, who was to become a close friend of mine for many years, knew more about *Alice in Wonderland* and Gilbert and Sullivan than cricket. He could recite and sing lengthy passages from both mediums, but scarcely knew the difference between a no-ball and a yorker. He soon learnt the rudiments of the game, though, and became a brainwashed disciple of Douglas Jardine. He wrote a book about the tour entitled *Jardine Justified*. My copy is signed, 'To Gilbert (who will hardly agree with a word of it!)'

The London *Evening Star* was represented by J.B. (Jack) Hobbs (afterwards Sir Jack), England's famous opening batsman, whose partner, Herbert Sutcliffe, was a member of the team. Jack was a lovely fellow traveller, modest, unassuming and good-natured. Although retired from Test cricket, he was still playing as a senior professional for Surrey under the captaincy of Jardine of all people. Jack was accompanied by his wife, a rather large and formidable-looking woman, but an absolute dear on closer acquaintance. Mrs Hobbs 'mothered' all of us and was very popular.

Jack had been given a 'ghost' in the person of Jack Ingham, a burly, extrovert young (Lancashire, I think) lad, a sporting journalist from the London *News–Chronicle*, which was in the same stable as the *Star*. The bodyline drama to come was an absolute bonanza for Ingham, who got many a front page story in the *News–Chronicle* out of it. He delighted in sending off stories about 'squealing Australians' and pulling my leg about it. Nevertheless, Jack Hobbs kept a tight rein on everything written under his name by his ghost writer. There was a good reason for this as, throughout the tour, Jack and Plum Warner were joint carriers of a cross they would have liked to have forgotten.

In a match against Surrey at the Oval only a few weeks before the team sailed for Australia, W.E. (Bill) Bowes, of Yorkshire, had bowled 'fast leg theory' against Hobbs, who did not like it. He walked down the wicket and remonstrated with the bowler, while the crowd howled for Bowes to be taken off. 'If this goes on, someone will be killed,' Hobbs remarked afterwards.

Warner was as indignant as Hobbs and wrote in next-day's *Morning Post* that Yorkshire had fallen from her pedestal and her great reputation had been tarnished by the incident. He went further in a later article in the highly regarded magazine, *The Cricketer*. 'Bowes should alter his tactics,' he wrote. 'He bowled with five men on the on-side and sent down several very short-pitched balls which frequently bounced head high and more. That is not bowling. Indeed it is not cricket and if all fast bowlers were to adopt his methods there would be trouble and plenty of it.'

Warner's embarrassment was compounded by the fact that tall, blond, bespectacled Bill Bowes was a member of the touring team and, strange to say, Warner had been a member of the committee who had selected him.

Hobbs and Warner were never allowed to forget the Oval incident and their angry reaction to it as the tour progressed and bodyline reared its ugly head. They both adopted the same attitude: they said and wrote nothing one way or the other. Warner's stock reply to all awkward questions, relevant or irrelevant on any subject, was: 'The golden rule I learnt at the Foreign office was never to interfere in the internal affairs of another country'.

I should mention here that, in addition to our Press quartet in the *Orontes*, we were joined in Australia by Captain E.W. Ballantyne, a South African journalist representing the Exchange Telegraph Company and my main agency rival.

I waited a few days for the ship and its passengers to settle down before making myself known to the top echelon of the MCC party. I was not out to sell myself personally but to explain the importance of the Reuter coverage to all the newspapers of Britain and elsewhere. To do my job properly, it was obvious that I had to gain the cooperation and confidence of the team and its managers. In reverse, it was obvious (or should have been) that the team and its managers would want me on side to report them and their doings in the most favourable and competent manner.

About the fourth day at sea, I spotted Douglas Jardine, the captain, reading a book in a deckchair. I thought this was an appropriate moment to make myself known to him. I knew very little about Jardine, he was not exactly a pin-up character in the cricket world and he did not court personal publicity. Other members of the team such as Maurice Leyland, Wally Hammond, George Duckworth, Harold Larwood, Hedley Verity and Herbert Sutcliffe were all household names but Jardine was comparatively unknown to me. I remembered him as a formal and undemonstrative batsman who was rudely barracked as 'Sardine' during the 1928–29 MCC tour of Australia. Such

A rare photograph of Don Bradman, aged 21, carrying the drinks as Australia's 12th man in the Second Test against England in 1928–29. He was dropped after scoring only 8 and 1 (on a sticky wicket) in the First Test.

English cricket writers at the First Test in Sydney. From left to right: Bruce Harris (London Evening Standard), J.B. Hobbs (London Star), Capt. E.W. Ballantyne, (Exchange Telegraph Co.), Gilbert Mant (Reuters) and Jack Ingham (London Star and News Chronicle).

McCabe (facing camera), Richardson and wicketkeeper Oldfield gaze in disbelief as Herbert Sutcliffe plays a ball from O'Reilly onto the stumps without dislodging a bail in the First Test at Sydney. Unperturbed, Sutcliffe went on from 43 to score 194.

ignorance, however, did not prepare me for the reception I was about to receive from him.

I drew up alongside him in his deck chair and said, 'Excuse me, Mr Jardine, I'd like to introduce myself to you. My name is Gilbert Mant and I am the Reuter representative with the team and will be with you throughout the tour.'

Jardine looked at me for a moment, then returned deliberately to his book for at least ten seconds, making me acutely embarrassed and uncertain of what to do. When he looked up again it was merely to say, 'I see'. No handshake. No offer to help me in any way he could. Just a cold stare. I tried to explain that I would be covering the tour for all the newspapers in Britain and overseas, but he was un-interested and obviously anxious to get on with his reading. The silence between us became unbearable so I muttered something or other and moved away, somewhat flabbergasted by his churlish attitude. It was not what I expected from a captain of England.

Well, he's a cold fish, I thought. I hope Plum Warner is more friendly. Warner was almost effusive.

'My dear fellow, how nice to meet you!' he said, shaking me warmly by the hand. 'I had heard that Southerton was making the trip, but you are just as welcome. We will do all we can to help you. When I was with the Foreign Office, we always made a point of being on friendly terms with the press. We can help each other and we shall.'

I did not mention my reception by Jardine as I intended to make another approach to him. Although maybe I can do without Jardine, I thought. On second thoughts, I'll have to try him again. Being offside with the captain won't get me anywhere. It won't get him anywhere, either, I reflected.

By the next time I approached Jardine I had learnt a little more about him, not only from my fellow journalists but from members of the team. The cricketers were a matey lot and did not seem to bear me any resentment for being an

Australian. They were well aware that I had the means to give them a good (or bad) press in their home-town newspapers. Many of them were to become my very good friends in the months to come.

Few of the players could tell me much about their captain, who was to be known to them as Skipper rather than Mr Jardine. They knew about his cricketing ability, of course, but his natural aloofness was reinforced by the wide social gap between amateurs and professionals in those days. 'He's a queer 'un,' Yorkshireman Maurice Leyland said to me, which just about summed him up. (This was in the days when queer meant only odd, strange or quaint.)

Those who had been members of the 1928–29 MCC tour of Australia with Jardine told me of the merciless barracking he had undergone from Australian crowds (as I had seen for myself at the time). They told me it had engendered in him a great hatred of Australians in general. The more he was barracked for slow play and jeered at as 'Sardine' and other uncomplimentary words, the more unbending he became. It was not in his nature to placate the crowds with a wave of the hand or a bat. It was a one-man war against the mob, to be renewed with even more intensity in 1932–33.

His biographer, Christopher Douglas, relates that during a match against New South Wales 'Patsy' Hendren said to Jardine, 'They don't seem to like you out here, Mr Jardine'. 'It's f------ mutual,' replied Jardine. The very sight of the scornfully imperturbable Jardine—the multi-coloured Harlequin cap on his head and the silk handkerchief knotted around his throat—walking towards the wicket sent crowds into a frenzy of booing and abuse. On one occasion, fielding on the outer near the fence, he turned towards the taunting crowd and spat on the ground in disgust at their behaviour.

Jardine is frequently referred to as a Scotsman but I prefer to call him an Anglo-Scot, a formidable enough mixture. His parents were both Scottish and he lived with an aunt in Scotland as a boy, but the rest of his make-up was solidly English.

It is convenient to insert here details about Douglas Jardine's life, some of which I read many years later in a biography, *Douglas Jardine: Spartan Cricketer*, by Christopher Douglas. I appear briefly in the book as Gerald Mant, but never mind.

Douglas Robert Jardine as born in Bombay, India, in 1900 during the height of power of the British Raj. His father, Malcolm Jardine, was a distinguished jurist who had been a brilliant cricketer in his youth. A contemporary of Ranjitsinhji, Fry and Warner, he had captained Oxford University and was regarded as a future player for England. However, he went to India to further his fortune at the age of twenty-four and remained there.

At the age of nine, little Douglas Jardine was packed off from India to Scotland to live in a mansion with his Aunt Kitty. By all accounts, he was not lonely or unhappy there but became a bit of a 'loner' and (some said) was painfully shy. Aunt Kitty's house became his holiday base during his rigid English public school class-system education at a private preparatory boarding school, Winchester College and Oxford University.

Cricket was in his blood; his father had imbued in him a great love of the game and he had a natural talent for it. He excelled at it, especially as a batsman, at school and university. After he left Oxford, he again followed a family tradition and qualified as a solicitor, though he was never to practise as such. He worked as a bank clerk and in commercial firms, but cricket was his passion. Apparently he had no great ambitions in life beyond it.

In county cricket, he became known as a patient and redoubtable batsman and topped the national batting averages in 1927. He became captain of Surrey, was selected in the MCC team for the 1928–29 Australian tour and took strike for the pinnacle of his ambition as captain of England in 1931. With the 1928–29 barracking incidents in mind, there was doubt in some cricket Establishment minds about the wisdom of putting Douglas Jardine in command of the MCC team for Australia in 1932–33. His old Winchester cricket coach remarked that Jardine would make a good captain 'but he might lose us a dominion'. He was very nearly right.

So, with new information in hand, I made a second attempt to seek Jardine's cooperation with the same result as the first one. He made it quite clear by his attitude that he did not wish to have anything to do with me socially or officially. I was not wanted on voyage or anywhere else, for that matter. It was as if he regarded me as a cuckoo in the nest, an Australian mole in the English camp. To the best of my recollection, Jardine spoke only those two words—'I see'—to me directly for the next seven and a half months. We travelled in the same ships, the same trains and buses, stayed at the same hotels together, and he ignored my existence. When I was married at the end of the Australian tour, he was the only member of the English party who did not offer us congratulations.

I could not understand it and it hurt me deeply. The only reason I have ever been able to fathom for it was that I had committed those two unforgivable sins in his eyes—I was a journalist and, worse still, I was an Australian. This ostracism made my job exceedingly difficult and I was forced to depend on Warner and other members of the team for vital information and background briefing.

Bill Bowes and I were friends. He liked and admired Jardine and often on train journeys or in hotels he would say in his lovely Yorkshire brogue, 'I can't understand why you can't get on with Skipper'. 'Billy,' I would say, 'I can't understand why Skipper can't get on with me. I need his help badly.' We would argue about it but neither of us could give a satisfactory answer to the question.

Douglas Jardine has been variously described by his critics as being reserved, taciturn, detached, cold, indifferent, aloof, authoritarian, stand-offish and frigid. He was all of these things to me. I was never given the opportunity by him to see the other sides to his character. His friends (yes, even Hitler had a mother) spoke of his charm, wit and intellect. Maybe I should have tried harder to breach his reserve but I didn't see why I should have to cringe to him in that way.

Warner was to say of Jardine, 'He is a queer fellow. When he sees a cricket ground with an Australian on it, he goes mad.'

Bob Wyatt, the vice-captain, said, 'Douglas was a strange chap. He was a sort of Jekyll and Hyde. He could be charming but he disliked the Australian, which was unfortunate.'

Gubby Allen also used the Jekyll and Hyde analogy, adding, 'When the Test matches were on he was insane, utterly determined to win at any cost'.

The disclosure earlier this year of Allen's letters to his father and mother at the time (sold at auction to the State Library of New South Wales for $23,000) astonished me by their virulence. We all knew that Jardine and Allen did not get on well with each other, either on or off the field, but no-one suspected that Gubby nourished homicidal tendencies towards his captain.

'Darling Dad, Douglas Jardine is loathed,' one of the letters said, 'and between you and me rightly, even more than any German who ever fought in any war.'

'Darling Mum, It won't be me so don't worry but sometimes I feel I should like to kill Jardine and today is one of those days.'

The letters must have been of particular comfort to Harold Larwood, living peacefully and happily as an expatriate in

Sydney. Harold bitterly resented being cast in the role of a
'killer' in the sensational Australian press. And nobody was
less like a killer than quiet, modest, likeable Lol. Now it
appeared that the real would-be killer was Allen of all people.

I never wanted to kill Jardine; I did not know him well
enough for that kind of thing. I just resented the fact that
he would not help me in my job.

The heading for this chapter—'The Unspeakable
Jardine'—is, of course, intended to convey the fact that he
did not speak to me for seven and a half months. Readers
who interpret in some other way are entitled to do so.

The *Orontes* headed for Colombo where we were to play a
one-day game against Ceylon (now Sri Lanka). Everybody
(except DRJ, of course) got to know each other better. Life
at sea for five weeks on a luxury liner in those days created
a little floating world of its own. Cliques were formed. Feuds
were begun. Romance blossomed. Gossip was rife and
everybody knew what everybody else was doing, or thought
they did. As expected of first-class passengers, we all
squeezed into our dinner jackets at night, with stiff starched
shirts and collars. It was stifling in the tropics, with no air-
conditioning, and as soon as dinner was over, we shed them.

The amateur and the professional cricketers were inclined
to keep to their separate selves. These were the days when
the social gulf was almost unbridgeable. The idea that a
professional would someday captain England was
unthinkable. Amateurs came out of one pavilion gate for
'GENTLEMEN', professionals out of another for
'PLAYERS' at Lord's and other major cricket grounds. I
once saw ten professionals solemnly take the field from one
gate at a county match followed (or preceded) by one solitary
'gentleman' from another gate. Scorecards and newspaper
reports of matches emphasised the distinction by giving
amateur players their initials while the pros received only

their surnames. Strangely, all Australians were regarded as gentlemen and identified with their initials. *Wisden* was still identifying the gentlemen as 'Mr' into the late 1950s.

Jardine did not extend his ostracism to the other two Australian-born members of the party. Gubby Allen, my old next-door-neighbour at Marathon Avenue, and Bill Ferguson, the scorer and baggage master, were acceptable and not regarded as Australian moles.

I had made myself known to Allen. He could recall little, if anything, about Marathon Avenue and Breakneck Steps but from then on we were on cordial terms. Gubby was a fine and energetic fast bowler, to achieve fame for refusing to bowl bodyline, not because he was Australian-born but because he thought it 'wasn't cricket' and was bad for the game.

On the other hand, Bill Ferguson was a fair dinkum Aussie of the old school whom it would be impossible for anybody to ostracise. Besides, Jardine wanted his laundry back.

Sydney-born Bill, or Fergie, had made a profession of scoring and looking after the baggage of international cricket teams for more than twenty years when I first met him. He had travelled the world with Test teams of England, Australia, South Africa, New Zealand and the West Indies. His scoring methods were unique at the time and probably done by computer now. He was the pioneer of charts showing the direction and value of every stroke by every batsman. In the press box he quickly answered questions about the number of singles, fours or sixes and times at the crease by all batsmen and every possible bowling statistic. His scorebook was immutable and the scoreboard operators were frequently brought into line.

Plum Warner called him our 'director of transport' as he shifted our mountains of luggage and cricket equipment on and out of ships, trains, buses, hotels and cricket grounds. Legend has it that the only piece of baggage he ever lost was his own. It was said that if Fergie had been Napoleon's master of baggage, the retreat from Moscow would have been a much more orderly affair.

Fergie also attended to our travel arrangements and needs for tickets to theatres or picture shows or other off-field entertainment. And our laundry, which was collected and delivered back as if by magic wherever we stayed. He had an 'arrangement' with all the principal laundrymen, black and white, of the cricket countries of the world and no doubt with hotel commissionaires and other go-betweens dependent on his patronage. We all paid him for his services, of course, and with his MCC contract he made a comfortable living out of it. A small, tidy man whom we all loved, Bill Ferguson was a friend and confidant of all the great cricketers and cricket writers of the world, with a wealth of cricket stories. Most of them were off-the-record and unprintable.

It has been said that the bodyline plot, cooked up in the grill room of the Piccadilly Hotel, was further stirred up on the *Orontes* during the voyage to Australia. Larwood wrote that leg theory was discussed several times at sea and that every member of the team knew what the tactics would be. 'We were asked to keep it quiet when we arrived in Australia so that we could give Bradman and the other Australian batsmen a surprise,' he wrote.

However, other members of the team are on record as saying that they were not privy to such discussions. I certainly knew nothing about it but apparently Bruce Harris did. 'The Larwood attack was evolved aboard the *Orontes* on the voyage out,' he wrote after the tour. 'Discussions were held at sea and practical experiments on land when the tour began.' Perhaps Jardine had already taken Harris into his confidence and pledged him to secrecy. As a mole, I was not included in the secret.

I was blissfully unaware of the calamity that awaited me in Colombo, capital city of Ceylon, a large island off the boot of India. Ceylon was annexed by Britain in 1796 and remained under British rule for more than 150 years until granted independence as Sri Lanka in 1948. The country became famous and rich through its exports of tea and rubber. One of the abiding legacies of the British presence was, and still is, the popularity of the game of cricket. It grew into a tradition with several well-known Ceylonese families. The De Silvas we played against in the one-day match in 1932 are still represented in Sri Lanka Test teams of today.

I felt very important, although a trifle nervous, as I was ushered into a reserved seat in the press box at the Colombo Cricket Ground for my first assignment. There was nothing much at stake in this match but Reuter had budgeted for a brief report with detailed scores. The players welcomed a chance to get rid of their sea legs and put in some practice.

I was glad to see that there was a cable company man in attendance to send Press messages off to London and elsewhere. Bruce Harris and Jack Ingham had indicated that they would be filing 'colour' stories about the game, secure in the knowledge that Reuter would be handling the scores and other statistics. There was plenty of colour to report—a large and vociferous crowd in a lush tropical setting with both sides playing light-hearted and entertaining cricket.

I was so raw at cricket reporting that I made an elemental mistake. I did not attach any significance to the fact that the official scorers were stationed on the opposite side of the ground, a little distant from the somewhat crude scoreboard which was operated by two rather excitable Ceylonese youths. If the scores were changed hurriedly on occasions, I did not notice at the time.

I thoroughly enjoyed the game and after it was over I strolled across the ground to the scorers' enclosure for a yarn with Bill Ferguson. Highly pleased by my performance, I had sent a nice little story about the match and got it off quickly in good time for the later editions of the London evening newspapers. Then, horror of horrors, a check with Bill revealed that some of my scores, including the totals, were wrong. In my ignorance, I had taken the scores from the scoreboard at times when the excitable young scorers had got it wrong.

I was aghast and raced across the ground just in time to catch the cable man and despatch urgent corrections. But I knew the damage had already been done. An hour had passed before the corrections could reach London and by then many scores would have been printed, not only in London but in other parts of the world. I tried to imagine the consternation in the Reuter office but it was beyond imagination. Serious mistakes in the first match by their new cricket correspondent whose appointment was already controversial and the ignominy of having to make corrections. What if it had been a Test match? (There were no regular England–Australia airmail or passenger services in those days and it was a few weeks before I learnt the truth in a private letter from a Reuter colleague in London. The affair had caused a minor crisis and serious thought given to my immediate recall. I could sense the office headlines: SEND FOR SOUTHERTON!—SOUTHERTON TO THE RESCUE! But a replacement by sea would take too long and be too costly. And flying was considered so risky in those days that the MCC imposed a general ban on flying by all members of the party. Anyhow, I was given a chance and one, as you will see, I did not let get away from me.)

The Colombo affair taught me a lesson I never forgot: never leave the scorers and, in particular, never leave Mr William Ferguson.

We stepped ashore at Fremantle, Western Australia, on 23 October 1932, most of us totally unprepared for what lay ahead. Three days later Douglas Jardine celebrated his thirty-second birthday with a party to which, needless to say, I was not invited.

6

A Word Is Coined

I do not intend to deal with the bodyline tour in detail; cricket buffs have read it all over and over again in fifty or more books and studies about the affair. I want to concentrate on the week in Adelaide in January 1933 that brought it to a head and the personal dilemma that faced me as the Reuter–Press Association correspondent.

Sixty years later, the story can be told with hindsight to a new generation of readers wondering how on earth the game of cricket could have caused major sporting and diplomatic upheavals that rocked the British Empire, involved the Australian and British governments and put a new word into the dictionaries. For any history of the 1930s has to include bodyline, along with the Great Depression, the rise of Adolf Hitler, the abdication of King Edward VIII and the outbreak of World War II.

Plum Warner set the ball rolling in an interview with the Australian Press after we filed ashore from the *Orontes*. 'The very word "cricket" has become a synonym for all that is true and honest,' he said:

> To say that it is 'not cricket' implies something underhand, something not in keeping with the best ideals. There is no game which calls forth as many high attributes, which makes so many demands on its votaries, and, that being so, all who love it as players, as officials or spectators must be careful lest anything they do should do it harm.
>
> An incautious attitude or gesture in the field, a lack of concentration in the committee room and a failure to see the other side's point of view, a hasty judgment by a spectator

and a misconstruction of an incident may cause trouble and misunderstanding which could and should be avoided. This is the aim of the Marylebone Cricket Club, of which I am a humble if devoted servant, in sending teams to all parts of the world to spread the gospel of British fair play as developed in its national sport.

The Foreign Office could not have done it better, but these lofty sentiments were to take a terrible hammering in the weeks ahead. One wonders whether Warner had an inner inkling of what was to come and was trying to head it off.

While Warner was uttering these soothing platitudes, Douglas Jardine was firing the first shot in a running war with the Australian press. Local sports writers asked if the announcements of selected MCC teams could be scheduled to fit in with their publication times. Jardine tartly replied that he had not come to Australia to convenience the press; he would announce teams etc at his pleasure. Eastern Australian journalists pointed out that Perth was two hours behind Sydney in time. 'Mr Jardine, Sydney and Melbourne are waiting,' they said. 'Tell Sydney and Melbourne they can bloody well keep on waiting,' Jardine was supposed to have replied.

All this suited me admirably as it meant that Harris, Ingham and I would have first bite at all information from the MCC camp. (By then I had been taken back into the Reuter fold in London after the calamity of getting the scores wrong in Colombo.) It was of almost immediate benefit to me. I still have in my possession a copy of a Reuter daily editorial log dated 21 October 1932, reading:

> Our Special Correspondent with the MCC team in Australia (Mant) enabled Reuter to secure a fine scoop with the MCC team chosen to play against Western Australia in their first match of the tour in Perth. We had the message on the wire at 10.54 a.m. in time to get on the front-page of the lunch News and Standard. The Opposition had a message at 11.42

a.m. which said that the team would not be chosen till tonight.

It shows how fierce press agency competition was in those days.

The tour started off quietly enough in Perth, picturesque capital city of Western Australia. After a comfortable MCC draw against Western Australia, there was another draw against an Australian XI with the MCC well in command.

Don Bradman had come 2,000 miles to the West by train like a conquering hero for this fixture, accompanied by leading Australian cricketers, Jack Fingleton, Victor Richardson, Stan McCabe and Ernie Lonergan. The hero-worshipping crowds were shocked that Bradman did not score a century or two, but keen observers of either side attached little significance to his scores of only 3 and 10. The wicket was rain-affected and neither Larwood, Voce nor Bowes bowled in the match. Moreover, the twenty-four year-old Bradman was in poor health and upset after a row with the Australian Board of Control over a writing contract.

We set off by train for more than four months of practically non-stop cricket from one side of Australia to the other. We went from city to city, from bush town to bush town, civic reception after civic reception, given by local mayors with chains around their necks. Musical welcomes with 'God Save the King' and 'For They Are Jolly Good Fellows'. And Plum Warner uttering platitude after platitude about 'cricket' and 'British fair play' until the subject became uncomfortable and undiplomatic.

Looking back, it's hard to pinpoint when the bodyline unpleasantness really began but the first real sign of it came in a match against an Australian XI in Melbourne. In the absence of Jardine on a fishing trip, vice-captain Bob Wyatt took charge and set a limited leg field for Larwood, Voce and Bowes, who got a haul of wickets. Wyatt, who did not approve of bodyline as such, is on record as saying: 'I do

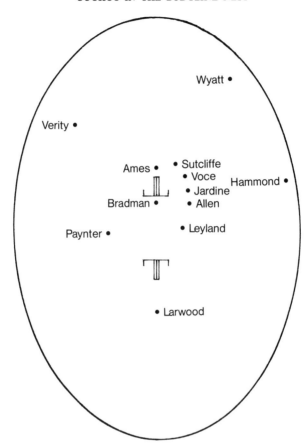

Larwood's bodyline field for Bradman.

not accept the blame for bodyline but I did set a leg side field in Melbourne but not with a view to intimidation. I was not in favour of a *short* leg theory attack with a concentrated leg-side field. Anything that breeds ill-feeling must be bad for the game.'

Jardine, back from his fishing trip, began to realise the potency of the secret weapon he possessed. The fast leg theory attack began to accelerate with *short* leg fields, with the deadly cordon of six or seven fieldsmen, and the crowds sensed it. Batsmen began to be hit and the crowds became restive, then ugly. The very sight of a bumper drew boos, to be redoubled when Larwood switched his early offside field to legside (usually in the third over). As the tour progressed, the booing became stronger and uglier.

Later in November we were reinforced by the large and jovial person of Maurice Tate, of Sussex. He had been delayed in England by illness. Known in some quarters as the 'spoilt darling' of English cricket, he was a favourite of newspaper cartoonists for his large hands and feet and buck teeth. Tate was undoubtedly one of the greatest medium-paced bowlers of all time. He was now past his prime at thirty-eight but, with a short run-up, could still bowl 'fizzers' that took off at great speed from the pitch. He was no slouch with the bat, either, and once scored a century in a Test against South Africa. It was Tate's third trip to Australia and it was to prove a very unhappy one. He bowled best with the new ball but there was just no way Jardine could give it to him when he had the services of Larwood, Voce, Allen and Bowes for the bodyline assault. Tate never played in a Test, saying sardonically that he was being saved for Wagga Wagga. He had always been very popular with Australian crowds and they gave him a bigger ovation than ever every time he took the field, blaming Jardine for their favourite's downgrading. Maurice was great company to travel with, though he became increasingly bitter towards Jardine.

Tate made a conspicuous debut against New South Wales in Sydney by taking 4 for 53, including the prized wickets of Bradman, McCabe and Kippax. Even that performance could not gain him a Test place. He never came to terms with it and became very disgruntled. That match was also notable for the fine first innings MCC batting total of 530. Sutcliffe scored 182, Les Ames 90, Wyatt 72 and Pataudi 61. The MCC won by an innings and 44 runs.

The First Test followed the match against New South

Wales and resulted in a handsome win to England by 10 wickets and one run. (Bradman did not play because of illness.) To the ire of the crowds at times, Larwood (10 for 124) and Voce (6 for 164) bowled leg theory but seven of their victims were clean bowled in a great performance by both of them.

A feature of the Australian batting was a swashbuckling 187 not out by young Stan McCabe. He took everything Larwood, Voce and Allen hurled at him with rare courage, pulling and hooking powerfully, though recklessly and a bit luckily at times. Nevertheless it was the sort of innings one remembers forever.

On the English side, Herbert Sutcliffe put together a patient match-winning innings though not without drama. When he was 43, a wrong 'un from Bill O'Reilly spun from the inside of his bat and onto the stumps, hard enough to rebound a foot away. Yet neither bail was dislodged from its groove (see photograph opposite page 65). The close-in fieldsmen McCabe, Richardson and wicketkeeper Oldfield looked on in disbelief. This apparent minor miracle did not disturb Herbert in the slightest, he was completely unflappable at any time. He continued batting as if nothing unusual had happened and went on to score 194.

The incident involved me in a temporary falling-out with Sutcliffe. During previous matches I had noted how he had several times given an early snick chance before going on to a big score. I was cheeky enough to suggest in a report that he must be 'one of the luckiest Test batsmen in history'. Some weeks later after the English mail reached us, Herbert confronted me with a batch of cuttings from Yorkshire newspapers carrying my report. He was more hurt than angry that a mere unknown cricket writer (an Australian at that) had dared to cricitise one of the greatest opening batsmen in the world. A certain coolness grew between us for a while until he laughed it off and forgave me. I was amused later

Pelham (Plum) Warner, the urbane but weak manager of the English team, was dominated by Jardine. When asked to comment on bodyline, Warner replied, 'Like Bismarck, I can be silent in seven languages'.

The deadly cordon of legside fieldsmen are foiled as the batsman ducks under a Larwood bodyliner during the First Test at Sydney.

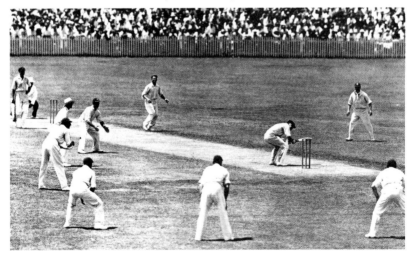

The power and majesty of a Bradman drive.

One of the huge crowds during the Third Test at Adelaide Oval when the bodyline crisis reached flash-point.

to read a piece about Sutcliffe by Arthur Mailey in which
he referred to

> an element of luck which one associates with that tenacious
> Yorkshireman was invariably on the door-step... His
> philosophical turn of mind will not allow him to become
> embarrassed when he gives a chance, no matter how simple
> that chance may be... The dour Yorkshireman with shining
> black hair and head erect looks nonchalantly around the field
> and continues batting as though nothing had happened.

Ray Robinson commented once that Sutcliffe almost made
the snick respectable.

The twenty-two-year-old Nawab of Pataudi literally batted
himself out of certain Test selection during the match,
although he scored 102. Up to that stage his batting had
been attractive and fruitful, 166 and 129 in Perth, 61 in
Sydney. But Pat (as we knew him) was obsessed with an
ambition to emulate his illustrious fellow Indians, the great
K.S. Ranjitsinhji, and his nephew, K.S. Duleepsinhji, who
scored centuries in these first Test matches against Australia.
This obsession was his downfall. His 102 runs took him a
laborious 366 minutes. During a period of 302 minutes when
he scored only 22 runs, Victor Richardson said to him
between overs, 'What's the game, Pat?' Pat replied breezily,
'Oh, I'm just getting the pace of the wicket'. 'Pat,' said Vic,
'the pace of the wicket has changed three times since you
came in.' Pataudi always blamed Jardine's personal dislike
of him for his absence from all the Test teams but I think
it was this unnecessarily slow innings that excluded him. He
was chosen for the Second Test in Melbourne but scored
only 15 and 5 runs. (There will be more about the Nawab
later in this book as we became firm friends and he promised
me an elephant as a wedding present.)

The Test ended on a somewhat farcical note. A late ninth-
wicket stand in Australia's second innings on the fourth day

carried the match into the fifth day. L. Nagel and W.J. O'Reilly were still batting at stumps with the score at 9 for 164, a tie with the English total. So we all had to turn up the next day at Sydney Cricket Ground, which was thrown open free to the public. Only one man took advantage of it and sat in solitary splendour on the Hill. We interviewed him and took his name but I can't remember it now. He was outnumbered by both teams and their attendants, umpires, gatekeepers, groundsmen, barmen, caterers, waiters, policemen, ground officials and the media. Voce clean bowled O'Reilly with his third ball without any addition to the score. Sutcliffe and Wyatt solemnly walked out to the middle to the ironic applause of the solitary figure on the Hill. Sutcliffe made a respectable snick off McCabe's first ball and the Test was England's.

The word 'bodyline' was coined during this first Test match in Sydney. There have been a number of claims for the title of its originator; I believe it was Hugh Buggy, as I have already stated. The word was never accepted in the English camp. Leg theory, or fast leg theory were the euphemisms used instead. Jardine was to say, 'What is this bodyline bowling? The word was coined by a sensational Press to explain or excuse defeat.' I had to conform; I do not think I ever used the term in my reports, except in parenthesis to denote a sort of dirty word.

Sir Richard Storey (see Acknowledgments) went straight to the top, the Marylebone Cricket Club at Lord's, for its version of the origin of the word. The MCC, in reply, quoted *The Dictionary of Cricket* by Michael Rundell (Allen & Unwin, London) as follows:

in November 1932 the *Australasian* (a Melbourne weekly) carried an article by Jack Worrall on the game between the MCC and an Australian XI, which had been played at Melbourne. Worrall's comments included the following:

Voce's half-pitched slingers on the body line provided about the poorest attempt at what should be Test bowling it is possible to conceive.

The controversy was already in full swing by the time Australia went in to bat at Sydney on the first day of the First Test (2 December 1932). Later that day, the *Melbourne Herald* (Australia's leading evening paper) carried a piece on the game that had been telegraphed from Sydney at lunchtime by its reporter Hugh Buggy. Echoing the phrase used earlier by Worrall, Buggy's article included the expression 'bodyline bowling' and this seems to have been the first use of the term. It is unlikely that Buggy's intentions were malicious—he was probably just using telegraphic shorthand for 'bowling on the line of the body'—but his sub-editor Ray Robinson kept the phrase intact. At any rate it was quickly taken up by the rest of the press, and it probably helped to raise the temperature of the debate.

Despite this, there are still shades of doubt about the matter. Rundell says Worrall (a former Australian international) wrote about the 'body line'. Jack Fingleton says Worrall wrote about the 'line of the body', which Buggy later telescoped into one word, and Ray Robinson popularised it in a headline. I give Buggy the verdict for his inventiveness.

7

An Immortal Ball

With the first Test in the bag, Bill Ferguson, having picked up his commissions from various laundrymen, hotel commissionaires and others, shepherded us and our baggage into the train for Wagga Wagga, a big country town in New South Wales. We were glad to leave the hullabaloo of Sydney behind us for a quiet rustic environment before the second Test in Melbourne a couple of weeks later.

If Maurice Tate was being saved up for Wagga Wagga, he did not make much use of it. Maybe he was already browned off by the realisation that he was never likely to play in a Test. At any rate, he took only one wicket in ten overs, though scoring a lively 52 not out with the bat. The star of the match was the little bespectacled Derbyshire coalminer, Tom Mitchell, the humorist of our party. Tommy's prodigious leg breaks completely bamboozled the country lads. He took 7 for 77 in the first innings and 5 for 26 in the second, including five stumpings by George Duckworth. Poor Tom! He knew, too, that even such a superlative performance would not earn him a Test spot.

We said goodbye to Wagga Wagga, entrained to Melbourne and then across Bass Strait by steamer to the island state of Tasmania, known to Australians as the Apple Isle, or Tassie. Two matches against Tasmania were played, one at Launceston and one at Hobart.

It was like old times when Jardine immediately became embroiled in a row with cricket officials at Hobart, except that this time even I had to agree that he was entirely in the right. The wicket was in an atrocious condition after heavy rain. The match was played after some protest by the MCC and Jardine aroused the ire of the spectators by refusing to risk his star Test bowlers, Larwood and Voce, in the mud. It was Christmas Eve and Jardine was barracked as a sort of Scrooge by bowling himself, little Lancashire left-handed batsman, Eddie Paynter, and batsman wicketkeeper, Les Ames, for forty overs. What's more, the MCC won by an innings and 138 runs.

It was a queer sort of Christmas, 1932, though the unseasonably cold weather, with light snow in Hobart and fires in the hotel grates gave it a slightly English atmosphere. The lads played some jokes on their leaders. Dirty Dick Palairet, a keen angler, walked into his hotel bedroom to find a fishing rod with a stinking dead fish on the end of the line dangling in a china chamber pot with liquid in it. Mr Palairet took it in good part and went up in our estimation. The Skipper found some toy tin soldiers pulling a miniature roller across the eiderdown on his bed. I can't recall the significance of it, but DRJ also took it in good spirits.

We stayed up until the early hours of Boxing Day to listen to the Christmas Day broadcast of King George V from Buckingham Palace to his British Empire. It was the early years of wireless and the shortwave static was bad but it aroused nostalgic feelings among the Englishmen. The husky, grandfatherly voice of the King, nearing the end of his life, had an emotional effect on all of us. The Royal Christmas broadcasts were to become a tradition carried on by his successors even after the British Empire existed no more. (Four years later, on 11 December 1936, I was to be with Gubby Allen's MCC team in a Brisbane hotel in the early hours of the morning listening to the abdication of King Edward VIII.)

We crossed turbulent Bass Strait again by steamer to Melbourne for the second Test with the gracious old Windsor

Hotel as our headquarters; it remains my favourite hotel of those days in Australia. The Test was not to be without all sorts of drama and the cables ran hot again, if cables do that sort of thing.

On Test eve Don Bradman and the Australian Cricket Board were once more at loggerheads. Bradman had an agreement to write about the Test for a newspaper group whose editorial director was Kerry Packer's grandfather, Robert Clyde Packer. Bradman insisted on honouring his agreement; the ACB issued an ultimatum that if he did so he would not play. Packer solved the impasse by releasing Bradman from his obligation so that he could play for Australia.

Jardine went into the Test with his full battery of fast bowlers—Larwood, Voce, Allen and Bowes—and by lunch on the first day it seemed as if it had been a tactical mistake. The wicket was slow and the scorching heat was tiring out the bowlers. The batting was slow and dull, too, and by 2.30 p.m. Australia was one wicket for 50. Thirty minutes later it was three for 67—Australia's captain, Bill Woodfull, bowled by Allen for 10, Leo O'Brien run out for 10 and Don Bradman bowled first ball by big Bill Bowes for a duck.

George Hele, the Australian umpire who stood in all five Tests, described the ball that bowled Bradman and the stroke he played as 'immortal'. Well, I don't know how you evaluate the immortality of a cricket ball and an errant stroke by the batsman. My dictionary describes immortal as being something that will be 'famous for all time', so I suppose that particular ball fits the word. (So would the ball that bowled Bradman for one of his other rare ducks at the Oval in London in 1948, only that ball was a very good one. It was to be the last Test ball of his illustrious career and he needed only four runs to finish up with an average of 100. Bradman played the first ball sent down by thirty-seven-year-old English slow bowler, Eric Hollies, off his back foot without scoring. The second ball was a wrong 'un, pitched slightly further up and whipping back from the off. It drew Bradman forward, he missed and was bowled. I guess that ball deserves immortality, too.)

Bradman had walked out to the wicket in Melbourne that day to the tumultous cheers of about 60,000 people confident that their hero was about to redeem himself with another one of his customary centuries. They gave no thought to his indifferent health or the trauma of his row with the ACB. Heroes are not immortal like cricket balls. Alas, heroes are mortal like the rest of us, and crowds are fickle by nature.

Bradman's first-ball sudden dismissal was something I will never forget. (Blue Greatorex had it in the cable to Reuter London a few seconds later.) The roar of applause as he walked to the middle; the hush as big, gangling Billy Bowes began his run to the bowling crease; the continued shocked hush as the ball hit the stump; the long, long, lonely walk back to the pavilion to the accompaniment of subdued, sympathetic applause; and the familiar head-high boyish Bradman grin, behind which, I was sure, was a grim determination that England would pay dearly for this indignity. If I sound a bit like an Australian mole, that's the way I felt at the time, but nothing of this ever intruded into my Reuter reports. I reported strictly what I saw, not what I thought.

The 'immortal ball' was generally described as a bad ball and Bradman's treatment of it as 'ill-advised' or 'rash', but there are inconsistencies in subsequent analyses of it. Here are some descriptions of the ball that may remain famous for all time:

Bradman: 'Bowes' first ball pitched short of a length and well outside the off stump, but aided and abetted by a faulty pull shot, hit my leg stump.'

Fingleton (batting at the other end): 'to my surprise I saw Bradman leave his guard and move across the wicket before Bowes had bowled the ball... Bradman was outside his off stump when the ball reached him. He swung at it and hit it into the base of the leg stump.'

Larwood (fielding at short gully): 'It was a shocking long hop and deserved to be clouted to the fence. That's what Bradman tried to do but I think he was a victim of the slowest wicket I have ever bowled on. The ball came off so leisurely that Don had already completed his stroke when it came off his bat. The ball just stopped against the wicket.'

Hele (umpiring at Bowes' end): 'Bowes' first ball to him was short and well outside the off stump. Crouching a little, Bradman stepped back a foot or more outside the off stump, his right leg bent almost at right angles as he pivoted almost square-on to the ball, now approaching his left shoulder. Swinging his bat horizontally and over the ball, he contacted it with the bat's lower edge and dragged it on to the base of his leg stump before he followed through. The bail on the middle and off stump did not fall... I have always regarded that stroke as a rash one. I am confident that he could have directed that delivery of Bowes anywhere he wished on the off side of the wicket through the virtually vacant field for four. But that is cricket and that ball and stroke will remain immortal.'

Mant: It happened so quickly and so long ago that I cannot remember what I saw at the time. But, examining photographs of the dismissal, it seems that George Hele was wrong in saying that only one bail fell. The photographs clearly show the leg stump at an angle and both bails dislodged. A minor thing, maybe, but it shows that memories can be unreliable at times.

Australia went on to compile only a mediocre total of 228, thanks mainly to a gutsy 83 by Jack Fingleton. Then it was England's turn to waver, the destroyers being W.J. (Tiger)

O'Reilly, who took 5 for 63, and fast bowler Tim Wall 4 for 52. England was all out for 169.

Australia's second innings was nearly all Don Bradman. He regained his super-hero status with 103 not out of a total of 191, an innings of innovation, brilliance and true grit. Some people still regard it as his greatest innings, considering the circumstances on and off the field. He demonstrated for the first time his method of trying to counter bodyline by stepping away to leg and cutting the ball to the off. It was fraught with danger to wicket and limb but it came off in Melbourne when it was needed most. Play was held up for some minutes when he reached his century as the crowd of 65,000 rejoiced. They organised a 'bob in' collection around Melbourne Cricket Ground to buy their hero a piano. Even Jack Ingham, who taunted me mercilessly about 'leg theory' and 'Our Don' had to pay tribute. 'He's a good 'un, all right,' he admitted.

England's second innings fell apart as their batsmen (except for Sutcliffe's 52) were mesmerised by the spin of Tiger O'Reilly, 5 for 66, and H. (Dainty) Ironmonger, 4 for 26. England totalled a mere 139 and the Test was Australia's by 111 runs.

Arthur Mailey said it was a 'victory of subtle spin bowling over shock tactics'. O'Reilly's haul of 10 for 129 set him on his way to becoming Australia's greatest ever bowler. A.G. (Johnny) Moyes rated him in the first four of all time, the others being Spofforth, Turner and Barnes. Bradman described O'Reilly as being the 'daddy of them all'. He believed that Barnes and O'Reilly were the two greatest bowlers who ever lived and that each was undoubtedly the greatest of his time.

There was only one fixture, against a Victorian Combined Country team at Bendigo, before the third Test at Adelaide and this was the only occasion during the tour when any real trouble loomed within the MCC party. Harold Larwood

had become the No. 1 star of the English team; gate receipts
dropped when he was not playing. Lol was the man
Australians loved to hate, although they overdid it so much
that Larwood began to hate them in return. I truly believe
that at heart they really liked him and wished that he would
bowl off theory instead of leg theory so that they could
applaud instead of boo him. I think a lot of the barracking
of Larwood was really directed against Jardine, who was
regarded as his evil genius.

Jardine exploited his No. 1 attraction for all he was worth.
He over-bowled him so much that Larwood finally rebelled
at Bendigo. Despite having bowled thirty-five overs in
scorching heat in Melbourne and having sore feet, he was
chosen as twelfth man for this minor match. It was too much
for Lol—he crossed his name off the list of players Jardine
had pinned to the wall of the Shamrock Hotel where we were
staying. This was an act of unbelievable defiance by a
professional cricketer in those days. In his book, Larwood
says the incident was widely publicised. I don't recall that
but I do remember that Bruce Harris, Jack Ingham and I
made a pact not to report the affair to England as we feared
it would involve Larwood in serious trouble with the MCC.

What may also have contributed to Larwood's impulsive
action was that Jardine, Warner, Palairet and all the
amateurs had been invited to spend the day with Major Alan
Currie at his station property, Ercildoune. Herbert Sutcliffe,
the senior professional who liked to regard himself as an
amateur at times, was also invited. The rest of the
professionals and we four pressmen (including Jack Hobbs)
were left behind to twiddle our thumbs or amuse ourselves
as best we could in the hotel bar or environs for the rest
of the day. You may argue that Major Currie was entitled
to offer hospitality to whomever he wished. Quite so, but
I still think it was thoughtless and in poor judgment by the
team's leaders to allow such a blatant act of social distinc-

tion to occur. One of the managers or an amateur should have stayed behind as a gesture or to see that we behaved ourselves. The exclusion of the pros and ourselves invited hurt and trouble. The trouble was not really bad but it was unfortunate. I've never spoken about it before and I am not going into details now.

To understand this situation, you must realise that our MCC party was in effect a small army detachment in the Bodyline War, operating in enemy territory. The managers and the amateurs were the officers and the professionals were other ranks and treated as such. We four pressmen were war correspondents, unarmed but with officer status. The distinction was hard to understand in egalitarian Australian eyes but the lines were sternly drawn. Discipline under General Jardine was as strict as he could make it without risking a mutiny.

Apparently Larwood was never disciplined by the MCC for his revolt, but the Skipper imposed his will with a Machiavellian swindle. Next day he persuaded the Bendigo cricket officials to bat thirteen men and the MCC twelve. And he made Larwood do his penance by bowling eighteen overs in the two innings, taking 7 for 44.

Jardine told Larwood he had taken the action to save him the embarrassment of being only the twelfth man. 'He knew that wasn't the reason for my objection just as well as I did but there was nothing I could do except play,' wrote Larwood.

8

The Battle of Adelaide

And so, one Test apiece, to Adelaide for the third encounter. The capital of South Australia, Adelaide and its beautiful cricket ground were the most unlikely setting for a donnybrook. It was known as the 'city of churches' and had a rigid social, cultural and cricket Establishment. Its people were said to be 'more English than the English'.

One fateful ball from Larwood brought everything to a climax in the afternoon of the second day's play before a crowd of more than 50,000 people. Stepping to his off, Australia's captain, Bill Woodfull, was hit heavily on the chest by the last ball of Larwood's second over and staggered back, dropping his bat. Larwood was bowling orthodox off theory to a slip field but the crowd was in no mood to differentiate between off theory and leg theory. All the incidents in previous games culminated into a violent eruption of booing and shouting.

There were to be extraordinary inconsistencies in the descriptions of that fateful ball by the main participants at the time and in later years.

Jardine said, 'With the last ball of his second over, Larwood brought the ball back from the *off* side and Woodfull, stepping outside his off side, failed to connect with his bat and received a nasty crack on his side'.

Larwood said the ball was a *straight* one.

And, believe it or not, umpire George Hele (at Larwood's end) said Larwood pitched the ball just short of a length on the *leg* stump. 'It rose sharply,' wrote Hele, 'and struck Woodfull over the heart. Woodfull jumped slightly in an attempt to get his bat straight over the ball. He did not duck... Jardine walked up to Larwood and said, "Well bowled, Harold". Larwood did not reply.'

Still shaken, Woodfull picked up his bat again and the roars of the crowd intensified as Larwood went to bowl the first ball of his next over and the offside field was suddenly changed to a legside one. Again there are vital inconsistencies. Jardine said Larwood made a sign to him that he wanted a leg-side field. But Larwood said, 'When I was on my way to bowl the first ball of my third over, Jardine stopped me in mid-stride and motioned the field over the leg-side'. Whoever initiated it, it was an injudicious and inflamatory action to take and both players expressed regret later. Jardine wrote, 'Had either of us realised the misrepresentation to which we were to be subjected, neither of us would have set that particular field for that particular over'.

In the crowd that day was cricket lover Robert Gordon Menzies, attorney-general of Victoria, later to become prime minister of Australia and Sir Robert Menzies. He was sitting next to 'Plum' Warner in the committee box and he takes Larwood's side in his memoirs, *Afternoon Light*. Menzies described how Jardine tactlessly complimented Larwood for his bowling after Woodfull was hit, and continues:

Gubby Allen, who was to bowl the next over, ran off the ground for a glass of water. After a minute or two, Woodfull stood up, but was obviously shaken. Then followed one of the most agreeable exhibitions of the true spirit of cricket which I have ever seen. Gubby bowled a series of almost long-hops, and Victor Richardson played them straight back along the pitch!

Then it was once more Larwood's turn, to Woodfull. An orthodox off-side field fell into place, Jardine at point. Suddenly Jardine signalled to Larwood and swung the field to the bodyline setting. It was almost as if he had said—'This man's groggy, let's dispose of him!'...

What happened thereafter is a part of cricket history; angry cables were exchanged; there was much bad feeling; all pleasure went out of the series. Jardine's action was a blunder of the first magnitude. He had in effect announced that bodyline was designed as a physical attack, no more, no less. Many years afterwards he confessed to me that he would like those five minutes over again!

The way Menzies described it was the way it appeared to me at the time, too. I was sickened by the apparent ruthlessness of it, though afterwards I fully accepted the published assurances of Jardine and Larwood that there had been no intention to take advantage of Woodfull's condition.

Be that as it may, I suddenly realised that this was not a game of cricket—it was a war. If it was allowed to continue, the main casualty would be the gracious and noble old game of cricket itself. It had nothing to do with being Australian or English. It did not matter whether Jardine was a bastard and Larwood was a nice fellow. The game of cricket was greater than them and greater than the rowdy, biased barrackers and all the other rights or wrongs. The fact that it was all within the rules was immaterial. There was no doubt that bodyline bowling was meant to be intimidatory. Any bouncer or bumper, with or without a legside field, is intimidatory. Nobody in their right senses would suggest that it was the deliberate intention of the bowler to maim or kill a batsman, but the danger was always there. The ball was aimed at the body and statistics that so many batsmen had been clean bowled proved nothing. In fact nine Australians in the match were clean bowled, Allen taking 8 for 121 with old-fashioned off-stump bowling. Few had the agility and brilliance of Don Bradman to attempt to combat it by stepping away and striking to the off. The less agile, flat-footed batsmen had to stand there and take it and, protecting themselves, put up a catch to the hungry leg cordon placed there for that very planned purpose. There was another aspect of bodyline bowling—it was spoiling cricket as a spectacle and eliminating the use of some of the classic batting strokes.

I wondered what would happen in lower grades of cricket if bodyline took hold; in LCCC cricket, for instance. That big, burly young fast bowler of Barclays Bank, who sprayed the ball around wildly at any time, would most surely kill somebody.

But I was in a hopeless Catch-22 situation to do anything about it; an anonymous, unknown Australian, a mole in the English camp. Christopher Douglas was right when he wrote:

> The Reuters correspondent Gerald [*sic*] Mant, whose reports appeared in *The Times*, was Australian and therefore suspect in Jardine's eyes. His reports were comprehensive but strictly factual and impersonal, as was Reuters policy. So the British public knew virtually nothing of the atmosphere in which the Tests were played.

If I showed the slightest sign of taking sides about bodyline, or suggesting it was a threat to cricket, my reports would be censored and I would probably be replaced. That was when I felt that James Southerton should have been there instead of me. Southerton, writing under a by-line, would probably have been able to speak his mind about the general atmosphere, although I did not know what his attitude to bodyline would be. (Southerton was to make a scathing attack on bodyline, sight unseen, in *Wisden* in 1934. A summary of it appears in a later chapter.)

So, reluctantly, I joined Jack Hobbs in not rocking the boat, reporting the play and the general uproar with perhaps too much impartiality. It was rather awesome to think that I was the main reporter in the whole cricket world of these history-making events. My reports went to all British newspapers, with special services by me to India, South

Africa and the West Indies. Even to King George V in Buckingham Palace, who loved his cricket and sent a cable of congratulations to the MCC when the Ashes were won. In other words, I was to some extent leading the British public astray. It has been on my conscience ever since.

I regret that I can shed little new light on the mystery of the celebrated dressing-room scene after Woodfull was hit and his innings finished. A doctor had been summoned to examine him. He was lying on the massage table waiting for the doctor when Warner and Palairet called to express their sympathy.

Most versions of Woodfull's reply seem to agree that he said: 'There are two teams out there on the oval. One is playing cricket and the other is not. This game is too good to be spoilt. It is time some people got out of it.'

Warner and Palairet were too taken aback to reply. They left the room in embarrassment.

Not many hours passed before we of the press had the story of the encounter in the supposed privacy of the dressing room. I can't recall for sure who gave me the information; it did not seem to matter at the time. I think it was Claude Corbett of the Sydney *Sun* but he would not tell me who had divulged the story. I do remember that I quickly sought out Warner in his hotel bedroom for confirmation. At first he tried, though half-heartedly, to appeal to me not to send the story to London for the 'well-being of the team'. I told him everybody else had it and it was not worth my job with Reuters to withold it. Reluctantly, he agreed that it had taken place and I rushed the story to London. Most of us guessed the leak had come from Jack Fingleton, a professional journalist, but he flatly denied responsibility. In fact, the denial became almost an obsession with him for many years and eventually he publicly named Bradman as the culprit.

In his biography of Jardine, Christopher Douglas wrote:

It will probably never be known who leaked the story, Warner

Australian captain, Bill Woodfull, hit over the heart by an off-side ball from Larwood during the Third Test at Adelaide. The crowd erupted when the field was moved over to a bodyline setting while Woodfull was still groggy. The fieldsman is Gubby Allen and the umpire George Borwick.

Armed mounted troopers were in position to quell a possible riot when Oldfield was felled by a Larwood delivery during the Third Test at Adelaide. The ball was 'legitimate' but the crowd reacted in fury. The fieldsman is Gubby Allen and the umpire George Borwick.

The mere sight of the haughty and scornful Jardine, the multi-coloured Harlequin cap on his head and the silk handkerchief knotted around his throat, was enough to incite Australian crowds into a frenzy of booing and abuse.

said it was Fingleton, Fingleton said it was Bradman and Leo O'Brien (Australia's twelfth man) further complicated the issue by revealing in an interview with *Wisden Cricket Monthly* that neither Bradman nor Fingleton was in the room at the time of the exchange but that [former Australian Test players] Jack Ryder and Alan Kippax, who were both reporting the match in one way or another, were.

Here we have all the ingredients for an Agatha Christie mystery. Who *was* in the dressing-room that day? Poirot, even though he knew absolutely nothing about cricket, might have identified the guilty man. Perhaps he would have pointed the bone at Woodfull himself. After all, why should he have wanted to keep his indignation secret? Sooner or later, it would have to be said; why not straight out in public by the Australian captain himself?

The Australian Sunday papers were full of the incident and next day there was more tumult to come. It was desperately unlucky for the English team that Bertie Oldfield, the Australian wicketkeeper, had to be felled by a legitimate short ball from Larwood on the off stump. He swung around to hook it, missed, and the ball hit him on the temple. He left the field for X-rays and played no further part in the match.

It was not Larwood's fault and Oldfield publicly acknowledged it. But, coming so soon after the Woodfull incident, the crowd did not see it that way. The scenes that followed were unprecedented on a cricket field anywhere in the world. The crowd went berserk.

The Press enclosure was in front of the administration centre in the Members' Stand and the tumult around us was indescribable as even the staid 'more English than the English' burghers of Adelaide and their wives stood up booing and shaking their fists. It was said that the armed mounted police troopers were grouped outside the oval to quell any possible riot. I do believe that had one man jumped the fence that day, thousands would have followed him. I believe that had there been television in those days, the British cricketing public would have been shocked by what they saw and called for an early end to it all, irrespective of the rights and wrongs of bodyline.

The next development in the drama was a statement about the dressing-room incident by Plum Warner: 'Mr Woodfull has expressed regret for Saturday's incident to messrs Warner and Palariet. The incident is closed and we are now the best of friends.'

Not with Woodfull, they weren't. Bill Jeanes issued another statement on behalf of Woodfull: 'I did not apologise to Mr Warner for any statement I made. I merely told him there was not anything between himself and myself. I strongly repudiate any suggestion that I tendered any apology to Mr Warner for any statement I made.'

One would have thought this was the statement to end all statements but there was more to come and sensational stuff at that. At about midday Jeanes invited members of the press to his office. There he read out a cable that he said the Australian Cricket Board had sent to the Marylebone Cricket Club in London.

The contents stunned me, especially one word. I raced back to the press enclosure and cabled urgent-rate messages to London. The messages would get to the Reuter office in two or three minutes, a minor communications miracle in the days before satellites and the use of overseas telephones for press work. I alerted London with a flash cable—'ACB OFFICIALLY PROTESTED MARYLEBONE ANTI-BODYLINE TEXT FOLLOWS MANTREUT'.

The text of the cable was: 'Bodyline bowling assumed such proportions as to menace best interests of game, making protection of body by batsmen the main consideration, causing intensely bitter feelings between players as well as injury. In our opinion is unsportsmanlike. Unless stopped at once likely to upset friendly relations existing between Australia and England.'

I was rivetted by the word 'unsportsmanlike'. The English unsporting! All hell will break loose in England, I thought. It would be about 2 a.m. in London, still time to catch the stop-presses of the morning newspapers. I prayed that somebody at Reuters would recognise the importance and significance of the message.

Somebody did, I learnt later in the day, and so did Viscount Lewisham, president of the MCC. Journalists woke him up in his bed by telephone and, as I suspected, all hell broke loose. The ACB had added insult to injury. Not only had they sent a clumsy, tactless cable but, seeing it was 2 a.m. in England, decided to send it at reduced rates to be delivered when the MCC office opened at 9 a.m. Viscount Lewisham was being asked to comment on a distasteful message from the colonies many hours before he would actually receive it. In fact, *The Times* of that date carried a short news item: 'Viscount Lewisham, president of the Marylebone Cricket Club, when asked last night whether that body had received any cable of protest against leg-theory bowling from the Australian Cricket Board of Control, said, "As far as I know, they have not received a cable".' As it happened the cable was not delivered to the MCC until just before noon, about ten hours after the Reuter cable.

A congratulatory cable to me from Reuters later in the day made me aware that no representative of my rival overseas news agencies had been present at the Jeanes conference. By sheer luck, I had given Reuters its biggest news scoop since the assassination of Abraham Lincoln in 1865 and caused an angry British peer to be dragged out of his bed at two o'clock in the morning.

It was the beginning of a cable war between the ACB and the MCC, with both sides acutely aware of the massive amount of gate money at stake from record crowds.

It was five days before the MCC replied to the ACB and there were feverish behind-the-scenes manoeuvres on both sides. In the interim, England easily won the third Test by 338 runs. I remember two incidents in particular during England's second innings. Jardine opened the innings with Sutcliffe and scored a solid 56. It was said that he strode out into the middle deliberately wearing his multi-coloured Harlequin cap, so hated by the crowds, saying, 'I'll give the bastards something to shout at'.

Wally Hammond played one of his majestic innings, immaculate off and cover drives. He was 85 not out with a Test century in sight when one of the last overs came up on the fourth day. In either a desperate or inspired move, Woodfull gave the ball to Don Bradman, bowled only occasionally in first-class games. Almost immediately the somewhat stunned silence of the crowd turned into an almighty roar. Bradman's first ball was a rank full toss. Hammond contemptuously attempting to hit it out of the ground into the nearby Torrens River played it on to his stumps and departed the scene in high dudgeon. There was incredulity in the press enclosure that Hammond could have fallen for such a ball. It happened so quickly and unexpectedly that there was argument about whether it really was a full toss. Somebody insisted that it was a leg break and it was then that I performed one of the rashest and most courageous actions of my life.

'I'll go down and ask him,' I volunteered and departed for the dressing room. Wally, scowling, was still undoing his pads when I got there. 'I'm sorry to have to ask you this, Wally,' I said. 'But was that a full toss?' A moody man at any time, Wally exploded into a torrent of bad language. I was left in no doubt that it was a so-and-so full toss and would I so-and-so get out of his so-and-so sight as soon as so-and-so possible. I withdrew hastily and reported back to my colleagues, 'Wally says it was a full toss'.

The ACB–MCC cable war continued until 8 February when the ACB more or less caved in by withdrawing the word 'unsportsmanlike'. It became known much later that the first cable of 18 January had been hastily drawn up without the unanimous support of ACB members, though telephone and telegraphic consultations were held with members absent in other states. The two Queensland delegates, for instance, were not aware of the provocative wording of the cable until after it had been sent. Had a proper board meeting been held, the whole affair might have been handled more diplomatically and a lot of unpleasantness averted. It was bungled badly and the Australian cricket bureaucrats were easy meat for the wise and experienced heads of the MCC in the war of words. To the relief of the various treasurers, the tour continued.

For the record, the principal cables read as follows. MCC to ACB:

> We, the Marylebone Club, deplore your cable message and deprecate the opinion that there has been unsportsmanlike play. We have the fullest confidence in the captain and team managers. We are convinced they would do nothing that would infringe the laws of cricket or the spirit of the game and we have no evidence that our confidence is misplaced. Much as we regret the accidents to Woodfull and Oldfield, we understand that in neither case was the bowler to blame. If the Board wishes to propose a new law, or rule, the proposal shall receive our careful consideration in due course. We hope the situation is not now as serious as your cable message appears to indicate, but if it is such as would jeopardise the good relations between the English and Australian cricketers and if you consider it desirable to cancel the remainder of the programme we would consent with great reluctance.

ACB to MCC:

We, the Australian Board of Control, appreciate your difficulty in dealing with the matter raised in our cable without having seen the actual play. We unanimously regard bodyline bowling, as adopted in some games of the present tour, as being opposed to the spirit of cricket and unnecessarily dangerous to players. We are deeply concerned that the ideals of the game shall be protected and therefore appoint a sub-committee to report on action necessary to eliminate such bowling from all cricket in Australia from the beginning of next season. Will forward copy of committee's recommendation for your consideration and hope for co-operation in application to all cricket. We do not consider it necessary to cancel remainder of programme.

MCC to ACB:

We note with pleasure that you do not consider it necessary to cancel the remainder of the programme and you are postponing the whole issue until the tour is completed. May we accept this as a clear indication that the good sportsmanship of our team is not in question? We are sure you appreciate how impossible it would be to play any Test in the spirit we all desire unless both sides are satisfied that there is no reflection on their sportsmanship. When your recommendation reaches us it shall receive our most careful consideration and will be submitted to an Imperial Cricket Conference.

ACB to MCC:

We do not regard the sportsmanship of your team as being in question. Our position was fully considered at the recent meeting in Sydney and is as indicated in our cable message of January 30. It is the particular class of bowling referred to therein which we consider as not in the best interests of cricket, and in this view, we understand, we are supported by many eminent English cricketers. We join heartily with you in hoping that the remaining Tests will be played with the traditional good feeling.

As it happened, the final ACB cable, withdrawing the offensive 'unsporting' term, reached the MCC only two days before the start of the fourth Test in Brisbane in February. Just in time. Jardine had threatened to decline to take his team on to the field unless there was a withdrawal, and he meant it. So the ACB climbed down. They had lost the battle but were eventually to win the war.

Few of us were aware at the time of the intense political and diplomatic lobbying going on behind-scenes in Britain and Australia. It was years before the full story was told. A worsening of Anglo–Australian relations was the last thing the countries wanted during an economic depression. Yet bodyline bowling was even threatening the renewal of a large conversion loan to Australia.

Meantime Adelaide had become awash with journalists. The Australian sensational press excelled itself with stories of dissension in the English camp and one preposterous story of Maurice Tate throwing a glass of beer over Jardine, a complete fabrication. The Bodyline War was also being featured overseas, the Americans equating it with the 'bean ball' in baseball—a ball aimed at the opponent's head. The Australian gutter press cried 'Killers!' The English gutter press retaliated with 'Squealers!'

An incredible atmosphere of bitterness and acrimony marked that fateful week in Adelaide. Nerves were on edge, tempers were frayed among cricketers and the public alike. Relations between the two teams had soured, too, both on and off the field. No longer were there any traditional visits to each others' dressing rooms. To be an Englishman in Australia was hazardous. Social ostracism, even a punch on the nose, confronted Perfidious Albion at the mere mention of bodyline. It was sheer national hysteria.

There were at least forty newspapermen in Adelaide and few of us went to bed before the early hours of the morning. It was not safe. We were frightened of being scooped. Rumour chased rumour. As like as not, at 1 a.m. the hotel where most of us were staying would go into violent hysterics with the news that Jardine had committed suicide over Glenelg Pier, or that Bradman had signed up to play with Fiji during the coming summer, or that all shore leave had been cancelled in the British Navy, and other absurdly fantastic tales.

Throughout the tour we newspapermen were hounded from pillar to post. We faced explosive broadsides of invective from both sides. We wrote millions of words (my total quote of 25,000 words had long been exceeded). Adjectives burst like bombs around the press boxes. Sensation followed sensation. Larwood's sore foot had more news value than a blood purge, than 50 million Chinese drowned in Yellow River floods, than the fate of nations at Geneva.

It would be an exaggeration to say that our English party was one big, happy family, but there was no real dissension. Maurice Tate and the Nawab of Pataudi actively disliked Jardine and Gubby Allen, in those letters to his parents, said he sometimes felt like killing him. Moreover, many of the party were deeply concerned at the idea of bodyline being employed in English county cricket on their return home. All these jealousies and disappointments and doubts were forgotten for the time being in the face of adversity. We were a besieged party in a hostile camp and it drew us together.

There was complete unanimity when the team met and drafted a resolution of loyalty to Jardine and the MCC, as follows:

The members of the MCC England team have no desire to enter into public controversy, for they deplore the introduction of any personal feeling into the records of a great game. In view, however, of certain published statements to the effect that there is, or has been, dissension or disloyalty in their team, they desire to deny this definitely and absolutely, while assuring the public of England and

Australia that they are, and always have been, utterly loyal to their captain through whose leadership they hope to achieve an honourable victory.

I would have happily signed that, too, had I been asked, despite Jardine's antipathy towards me.

In the meantime, I had to ask Reuters for reinforcements. I was finding it impossible to deal single-handedly with scores, descriptions of play and never-ending off-field developments. Coverage of the actual play required practically ball-to-ball descriptions every ten minutes or so. A wicket fall had to be cabled without a second's delay, so fierce was the agency competition. I was given my old friend and colleague, E.N. (Blue) Greatorex, a distinguished Australian Rugby international and a tearaway fast bowler at cricket. Blue mainly handled the scores and was a huge help to me. By the reactions from London, I think we kept the Reuter flag flying high above the others.

9

The Lighter Side

It was not all mayhem and malevolence. I recall a rather droll incident in the Richmond Hotel in Adelaide when the turmoil was at its height. It involved Hedley Verity, the great Yorkshire left-hand, slow-medium bowler of immaculate line and length. Hedley was an abstemious, serious-minded fellow, whose head was often deep in books such as T.E. Lawrence's *Seven Pillars of Wisdom*. He was a member of a friendly society in Yorkshire which was somehow linked with the Rechabites. In case you don't know your Bible, Rechab was the father of Jonadab and refused to drink wine or build or live in houses, or plant or own vineyards. Modern Rechabites are total abstainers from intoxicating drinks.

There we were, the four of us, sitting in the hotel lounge with tankards of delicious icy-cold South Australian beer on a table in front of us. Myself, Hedley Verity, Tom Goodman *(Sydney Morning Herald)* and Jack Ingham.

A waiter approached Hedley and said, 'There are three gentlemen waiting outside to see you, Mr Verity'.

'Did they say who they were?' asked Hedley.

'Yes,' replied the waiter. 'They're from the Adelaide branch of the Rechabite Society.'

Well, you never saw such a scatter. The three of us whipped the four tankards off the table and fled to the darkest corner of the lounge. Hedley, with quick presence of mind, ordered a lemon squash from the waiter and awaited the arrival of the intruders. We watched three cadaverous-looking men with long beards approach him and sank his beer between us. I mention this incident only to illustrate that bodyline was such a deadly thing it could even drive a Rechabite to drink.

Some of us managed to get away from it all in Adelaide one Sunday for what could loosely be called a 'picnic' cricket match in a public park at Belair, in the Adelaide Hills behind the city.

It so happened that the Midnight Frolics theatrical company headed by English-born vaudevillians, Edgley and Dawe, were playing at an Adelaide theatre. Clem Dawe, a morose man at times off-stage as many comics are, was a marvellous comedian with a touch of Chaplin whimsy and pathos about him. Clem and Eric (Mick) were brothers and some of the Flanagan and Allen favourites such as 'Underneath the Arches' were in their repertoire. Mick's wife, with the stage name of Edna Luscombe, was stage manager, chorus mistress and what-have-you. Their son, Michael, was to become one of Australia's top entrepreneurs and Edna Edgley herself a legend with the Australian Ballet.

Eric and Clem, who came from the centuries-old English White family of theatricals, were both cricket fanatics and the back stage of the theatre became a haven from the turmoil of bodyline for certain members of the English team and press correspondents travelling with them. There was an hotel next door with a small window facing the back stairs of the theatre from which bottles of beer could be easily taken into the dressing rooms.

Clem would come off stage after singing lugubriously 'Ain't It Grand To Be Blooming Well Dead' for a reviver. Other customers were the Sun-Tanned Eight chorus girls and the 'juvenile' lead, dear old Alec Regan, who must have been at least forty at the time. There was mild chaos at times. I remember one night Bill Voce taking the wrong turning and finishing up in mid-stage with the Sun-Tanned Eight to the tumultous applause of a packed house, who recognised him. It was Big Depression times and laughs were precious.

Anyhow, the staff of the next-door hotel challenged the cast of the Midnight Frolics to a Sunday cricket match, the hotel to supply liquid refreshments and the company to supply the orchestra and entertainment. I shudder to think now that a large lorry was required to convey the amount of beer the publican considered necessary for a Sunday cricket match. Tom Goodman and I were selected in the Midnight Frolics team and my recollections of this memorable match are vague. I recall the inevitable mock bodyline attack on the publican by Clem Dawe, the slowest fast bowler in history, and the gradual deterioration of the orchestra as the day wore on, the throaty sound of the saxophones echoing unsteadily through the Adelaide hills. Tom Goodman, for some unexplained reason, wore a black top hat while fielding and batting.

I seem to recall the Sun-Tanned Eight sitting on the sidelines and knitting socks or something like young Madame Defarges at the guillotine during the French Revolution. I recall an agonised and futile cry of 'Catch it, Jack!' by the rest of our team as the ball sailed high in the air towards a stagehand lying supine in the outfield in a stupor. I recall clearly that Herbert Sutcliffe turned up to watch the match late in the day at the moment I executed a magnificent square drive to the boundary off the hotel's demon bowler. Herbert held me in much higher respect after that feat, despite my being clean bowled in attempting to treat the next ball in the same way.

After Adelaide, bodyline was not exploited with quite the same intensity. Games against Victorian Country at Ballarat, New South Wales at Sydney and Queensland at Toowoomba as a lead up to the vital fourth Test at Brisbane passed off in relative peace. The crowds retained their fury at the mere sight of a bouncer but there were no serious casualties that I can recall. At the civic receptions they still sang 'God Save the King' but we were no longer Jolly Good Fellows.

Our party was not exactly friendless. The amateurs were feted in their elite reciprocal social clubs and there were plenty of English migrant families in Australia to look after the professionals. A number of the cricketers actually fraternised and drank with convivial Australian newspapermen, though Skipper would have frowned on this. Despite his bitter on-field war with the crowds, Harold Larwood was to write, 'They can say what they like about the tour but I wouldn't mind another one as enjoyable'. Lol liked his beer and also liked a pinch of snuff during his bowling spells in the middle.

I had relatives and friends wherever we went. I was able to skite about staying in posh hotels such as the Windsor and the Australia instead of returning to the land of my birth, a failed welfare office to a bunch of pommy boy migrants. In addition, I had become particularly friendly with some of the players. They were all good blokes of very different character and upbringing but we were bound together in adversity and I was not regarded as a very dangerous mole.

Bob Wyatt, the vice-captain, and I had things in common and we talked together a lot. Bob was a music lover and his gramophone was constantly in play. So was his camera; he was a bit of an authority on films and film-making. Bob finished the tour with a creditable Test average of 46.71. He did not approve of bodyline but remained absolutely loyal to his captain throughout. We exchanged letters on the occasion of his ninetieth birthday in 1991, mine following in 1992.

I developed a firm, and I suppose unlikely, friendship with big Bill Voce, the Nottinghamshire coal miner whose round-the-wicket, left-hand, short-pitched thunderbolts were such a perfect complement to Larwood. Bill was a tall, huge man with ham-like hands. His bowling was angry and dangerous, yet off the field he was the perfect 'gentle giant', though rather frightening when stirred to sudden anger. I detected a certain grandeur and sensitivity about Bill that defied analysis and I believe that in another age he might have been a person of some eminence. Another good friend was that dour but humorous Yorkshireman, Maurice Leyland, a left-hand batsman of dogged brilliance. Bill and Maurice and I toured together again in 1936–37 and I remember both of them with affection.

Another unlikely friend was Iftika Ali, the Nawab (prince) of Pataudi, ruler of a small Indian principality south of Delhi. He was only twenty-two, eight years my junior, but it made no difference. He was a slim, volatile young man, an Oxford graduate of some distinction, with a quick sense of humour and fun. His eyes sparkled and his giggle was infectious.

The Nawab soon became Pat to everyone, even to barrackers, without him losing any dignity in the process. In an early match in Perth when he was fielding on the fence, a spectator asked, 'Do we call you Your Highness?' Pat shot back, 'Just plain Pat to you boys'—and he was their friend forever. They treated him more roughly in the eastern states but he won them over there, too.

The fact that Pat and I were both on the nose, so to speak, with Jardine may be one reason why we were drawn together. Another reason was that we were both fond of billiards, though he always won, being an Oxford blue at the game. We played many games together in sleazy billiards saloons, usually underground, in the capital cities. The only drawback was that Pat was immediately recognised and attracted a large crowd of onlookers gawking at the only Indian prince they had ever seen or were ever likely to see again.

Although Pat handled the barrackers well, underneath he was deeply hurt by some of their gibes, especially the racial ones. The crowds called him 'Potato', 'Pat O'Dea', 'Gandhi' and 'Gunga Din' and shouted 'Where's your loincloth?' He got his own back one day in Melbourne while fielding on the fence. 'Where's your goat?' a barracker shouted. (Gandhi was often accompanied by a goat for milk.) Pat peered into the crowd, pretending to recognise the offender. 'Ah, there you are!' he said. 'Would somebody lend me a piece of rope?' The crowd burst into laughter and applause. He once even had to withstand Jardine himself in Melbourne when he declined to move from the off to the legside as ordered for a bodyline attack. 'I see His Highness is a conscientious objector today,' Jardine said with heavy sarcasm. I think that Jardine's superior attitude towards Pataudi probably dated back to the days when he was a child of the British raj in India. At times he seemed to treat Pataudi as though he was a disobedient native servant. The dislike between them was intense.

Pat promised me an elephant for a wedding present but it never turned up. Alas, Pat and most of the 582 Indian princes lost their principalities and elephants when India and Pakistan gained independence in 1947.

The barracking was undeniably bad during the bodyline tour but there was provocation and most of the crowds knew their cricket. It was mild compared with what goes on today. Soccer barrackers in England and Europe actually kill each other. Australian Rugby league crowds can be very nasty, though in tennis the players are the louts rather than the spectators. It is unproductive to compare the scenes of 1932–33 with the disgusting behaviour of some crowds at the limited-over one-day games of today. The game is not the same, as Alan McGilvray wrote, and the crowds who watch it are not the same, either. Barracking is also taking hold in golf in America and Japan, a sad development for a game that has for so long been a model of sportsmanship by player and spectator alike.

Jardine copped some venomous barracking in Adelaide. 'Don't give him a drink, let him die,' a man shouted out as the twelfth man took drinks on to the field. 'Don't kill the flies—they're your only friends,' shouted another one as Jardine brushed the pests from his face. Australia's famous Yabba put it much more subtly when Jardine took similar action at Sydney Cricket Ground. 'Mr Jardine, you leave our bloody flies alone,' he pleaded.

Yabba still reigned over the celebrated Hill at Sydney Cricket Ground when we got there. He had become the game's most eminent barracker. He refined the old cries of 'Get a bag' when someone dropped a catch or 'Send for the fire brigade' or 'You couldn't hit the water if you fell out of a boat' to get a dull batsman out. Yabba gave his comments style and wit and his raucous voice could be heard from one side of the ground to the other.

His real name was Stephen Harold Gascoigne, a Sydney rabbit hawker. In a Sydney *Sunday Telegraph* story, Mark Gold told how Yabba would arrive at the Sydney Cricket Ground early, carrying a hamper which contained his lunch and two bottles of beer. There he would hold court on his sacred piece of grass, surrounded by a crowd of admirers ready to applaud his caustic or hilarious comments to the players.

On one occasion Australian Test batsman Charlie Kellaway was his victim for taking many hours to score only 70 runs. 'Charlie, old boy,' boomed Yabba, 'you'll be a better batsman in the next world where time doesn't count.'

Our own Maurice Tate was another target when his size 13 boots had to be replaced three times during our match against New South Wales. 'Thank goodness he's not a bloody centipede,' Yabba remarked.

Once he reprimanded umpire George Borwick, who stood for all five Tests with George Hele. Borwick raised his hand to signal the sightboard operator to move his board. 'It's no use, George,' Yabba boomed, 'you'll have to wait until playtime like the rest of us.'

Yabba is also credited with having bestowed the 'Johnnie

An unofficial Test match in the Adelaide hills in January, 1933, between the Midnight Frolics theatrical team (pictured) and a local hotel took much of the heat off the bodyline crisis. Standing top left is English comedian Eric Edgley. Gilbert Mant is second from right next to top-hatted Tom Goodman (Sydney Morning Herald). Seated second from left is English comic Clem Dawe, the Frolics captain, and at extreme right, George Thatcher (Sydney Labour Daily). The padded-up batsman is the 'juvenile lead', Alec Regan.

Harold Larwood contemplates treatment of his Achilles heel—the damaged left foot that ended his career as one of the greatest fast bowlers in cricket history—David Frith Collection.

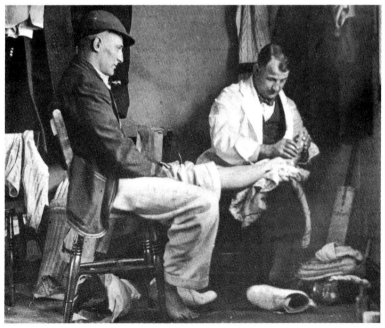

Sight-seeing at a hot spring resort in New Zealand (left to right) Gilbert Mant, Bruce Harris (London Evening Standard), Maori guide Kiri, Maurice Leyland, Tom Mitchell and MCC official scorer and baggage master Bill Ferguson.

A benevolent-looking Douglas Jardine nursing his baby daughter in Scotland some years after the Bodyline War.

Won't Hit Today' nickname on English captain J.W.H.T. Douglas. Jack Pollard tells how Yabba once shouted out 'Mind your stays, old man', as Jardine chased a ball to the outfield in his stiff-legged way. He says Yabba referred to himself as 'the one and only' and that his rich vocabulary owed a lot to his service as a soldier in the Boer War in South Africa.

The historic grassy Hill at Sydney Cricket Ground is now no more—it was removed in 1991 to make way for yet another sporting concrete jungle. Stephen Gascoigne, the rabbit-oh, did not live to see the desecration but his spirit is enshrined there in a brass plaque and the section in front of the scoreboard is officially named Yabba's Hill. Residents in nearby areas swear that sometimes at night they hear a raucous cry of 'Get a bag!' echoing like a banshee across Centennial Park towards Bondi.

The success of England's fast off and leg theory attack meant that there was little alteration to the sides chosen for the five Tests. This left a group of six players mostly on the sidelines. They were Pataudi (played in two Tests), Bowes (one), Mitchell (one), while George Duckworth, Maurice Tate and Freddie Brown were overlooked for all Tests.

These discards satirically called themselves the 'Ground Staff' and even had a special necktie designed and made with the image of a rabbit on it. They probably held secret ceremonies from time to time. Pataudi and Tate were disgruntled about their axing, feeling that they should have been selected, but the others took it philosophically and pragmatically.

It must have been a hurtful blow to George Duckworth in particular, who had for so long been England's premier wicketkeeper. He took it like a true sportsman. The inimitable 'Ducky' was an astute student of the game and would have understood the thinking behind his rejection in favour of Leslie Ames, of Kent. Jardine wanted Ames for his batting rather than his 'keeping' (in fairness to Ames, he went on to develop into one of the most outstanding batsmen–wicketkeepers the game has known).

Duckworth, a Lancashire lad, had become a legend for his stentorian and boisterous appeals behind the wicket. His anguished or angry 'Howzats?' could be heard far beyond the cricket grounds of the world. The crowds barracked every appeal but there was no venom in it and they loved him just the same. Short but bulky, George hurled himself at the ball like a contortionist, sometimes seeming to be tangled up with his pads. He was not the polished glove-man of the Bert Oldfield–Don Tallon type, but he was very quick and effective. He kept wickets against Australia in ten Tests, stumped three and caught twenty-three victims. George Duckworth was great fun to travel with and he had a host of friends in Australia. (I always regarded Ron Saggers as being among the best of them all and he was a brilliant batsman as well. He was understudy to Don Tallon with Bradman's 1948 tour of England and top 'keeper for Australia in the 1949–50 tour of South Africa. George Duckworth sometimes put on a tumbling act; Ron's glovework and movements always had the artistry of a ballet.)

Of the Ground Staffers, Bill Bowes could content himself with the knowledge that, although he had played in only one Test, he had bowled Don Bradman first ball. The ball was declared immortal and Bill would live with the glory of the moment for the rest of his life.

F.R. (Freddie) Brown was a twenty-two-year-old Cambridge graduate, a few months younger than Pataudi and therefore the youngest member of our party. Freddie was like a big, chubby-faced overgrown schoolboy and had been selected as a leg-break bowler and powerful batsman. There was no place for leg-break bowlers in this team and he was mostly used as a very competent twelfth-man drinks waiter. Freddie's cheerful nature did not allow him to go down in the dumps about it. If he did not have to perform on the field, he had a whale of a time with the Australian 'social set' off it. And Freddie had the last laugh. Eighteen years later, at the age of forty, he led the 1950–51 MCC team to Australia and came close to regaining the Ashes for England. In winning the fifth Test, he captained the first English Test team to beat Australia in twenty-six Tests.

10

The Ashes Regained

We went into Queensland after a comfortable four-wickets win over New South Wales in Sydney. Then followed a bit of a romp against Queensland Country at Toowoomba, one of the most pleasant and picturesque towns in Australia.

Play was endangered for a while when local cricket officials wanted to deduct a government entertainment tax from the MCC's share of the gate receipts. Treasurer Mr Palairet would have none of it and threatened to forbid the English team to take the field unless the full money was paid. Dirty Dick got his way and the meagre £3 involved was forthcoming.

Play got under way and the country boys were allowed to bat twelve. This allowed Larwood to take 8 wickets for 28 runs in 11 overs, all clean bowled. It seemed to me that the bushies were terrified of him before they even got to the wicket but it was a fine performance just the same.

There was a game scheduled against Queensland at Brisbane before the vital fourth Test. So we took up residence in the Bellevue Hotel, a fine old country-type hotel with long, wide wooden verandahs. Although it did not have all the 'mod cons' of the swanky pubs of Sydney and Melbourne, it was to be one of our favourite places on the tour. I would have thought that the old Bellevue was worthy of historic preservation but it has long since gone to the demolishers, like all rare old things and people.

One of the reasons for us liking the Bellevue so much was the presence of the licensee, Mick Maguire, and his wife and their three beautiful teenaged daughters. We all became a happy family with the Maguires. Mick was a retired professional pugilist who still packed a considerable punch. The three girls were nubile beauties who used to race along the hotel verandahs in the early morning rather scantily clad, shouting and giggling. It was said that Jardine took a shine to one of them. The fact was that we all took a shine to all of them. The eldest daughter, Mary, went on to became a film actress, Carmel married an English peer and I can't remember the name and fate of the third one.

Mick's pugilistic skill came in handy one day in a dramatic gun incident in the hotel's small private bar. The affair had nothing whatever to do with cricket or bodyline but came from nowhere.

In his book, Harold Larwood describes how he, Bill Voce, Les Ames and Tommy Mitchell were having a quiet drink, with Mick in the chair. Harold has forgotten that there were two others present, myself and big, beefy Tom Lawton, Australia's international Rugby union fullback of the day. I'm pretty sure George Duckworth was there too. Harold is right in recalling that a big, bearded stranger walked into the bar and started needling little, bespectacled Tommy who, fortified with a beer or two, removed his spectacles and foolishly shaped up to the intruder. Suddenly the big stranger produced a large revolver from his pocket and brandished it in the air. I can't remember whether it went off but we did. Harold says he vamoosed. I went under the bar, while Mick flattened the stranger with a perfect right cross. I suppose Tom Lawton tried to tackle him. It was just another one of the peculiar things that happened during the Bodyline War.

Main interest in the match against Queensland was the appearance of Eddie Gilbert in the local team. We were all curious to see this twenty-five-year-old black Aboriginal fast bowler who had achieved everlasting fame by bowling Don Bradman for a duck in December 1931. Gilbert had the reputation of being one of the fastest bowlers who ever lived. He was of only slight, but wiry build, with unusually long arms and a shock of thick black hair. With a run up of only four or five paces, he delivered the ball at sizzling speed. His bowling was often akin to his moody, unpredictable, though generally unassuming nature, but when he was on target, he was lethal. He said boomerang throwing helped to develop his right shoulder and wrist. There was much controversy during his career as to whether he was a 'chucker'. Slow-motion photographs proved inconclusive but umpire Andy Barlow no-balled him eleven times in three overs in Melbourne in 1931.

The over Gilbert bowled against Bradman in 1931 is Queensland cricket folklore. Bradman played the first four balls then was out on the fifth, caught behind. He later said that Gilbert was the fastest bowler he had ever faced. Of the chucker argument, Bradman said, 'If he did not actually throw the ball, he certainly jerked it'.

While playing for Queensland Gilbert lived in a tent in the backyard of the Queensland Cricket Association secretary's home in Brisbane, under an agreement with the Queensland Protector of Aborigines. Eddie Gilbert retired with a first-class bowling average of 87 wickets at 28.97 runs.

He disappeared from view for many years after his retirement, becoming a sort of legend. Fanciful stories were told about him doing a tribal dance at the wicket after bowling Bradman and of being a giant of a man, neither story having any substance. He was 'rediscovered' in 1972 in a mental hospital where he had lived for twenty-five years and was incapable of speech. He died in 1978, aged seventy. It was a sad ending for a fallen star.

Gilbert certainly sent down some thunderbolts during the MCC–Queensland match of 1933, one of them dealing Douglas Jardine a terrific blow on the hip. He took only 2/96 but loyal Queensland supporters claimed that poor catching robbed him of more wickets. He clean bowled Leyland for two and got Paynter lbw when he was 19.

I have to say here that details about Eddie Gilbert have come from Jack Pollard's prodigious encyclopaedia of cricket and cricketers, *Australian Cricket*, a masterpiece of sporting research.

And so the stage was set, as the cliche goes, for the Fourth Test at Brisbane, with English leading two Tests to one. A win for England and the Ashes were won. The atmosphere in the Bellevue Hotel was stern. Jardine & Co. had other things on their minds than the Maguire sisters bouncing up and down the verandahs on the morning of 10 February 1933.

The match was played at the Woollongabba ground, popularly known as 'The Gabba', and went into the sixth day, with Sunday as a rest day. The cricket was very dull at times but there was drama in plenty with sudden batting collapses by both teams. The weather was very hot and the wicket unresponsive for fast bowlers.

Australia got off to a great start with an opening partnership of 133 from Woodfull (67) and Victor Richardson of South Australia (83). At three for 233, Australia looked to be in a sound position, then the next seven wickets fell for 107 runs for a total of 340. The pattern was repeated in England's first innings on the third day. Jardine (46) and Sutcliffe (86) had put on 114, the best English opening partnership of the tour. The next six wickets went for only 150 runs and there was sudden crisis.

It was not the score of 8 for 264 so much as the condition of E. (Eddie) Paynter, the diminutive left-hand Lancashire batsman who was due to bat next. Paynter had fielded throughout the first day in the scorching heat. He had been suddenly stricken by tonsilitis and heatstroke and was now in bed in Brisbane hospital with a temperature of 102 degrees.

Eddie was a cheerful lad from the Lancashire town of

Oswaldtwistle, a name as funny to Australians as Wagga Wagga is to English people. There seemed no possibility that he could bat, or even take any further part in the match. The 'little 'un', as his team mates called him, had other ideas—and so had Skipper.

'Eddie will bat if he possibly can, even though on crutches,' Jardine had told Bruce Harris earlier, and so it proved. The little 'un walked slowly to the wicket, a white scarf around his neck and a wide sun hat on his head, and took guard. He stuck around until stumps for 94 minutes making 24, at one stage scoring only nine runs in 40 minutes. Twelfth-man Freddie Brown took him out tablets and a gargle during the drinks intervals.

Larwood wrote that Bill Voce was mainly responsible for getting Paynter to the ground. 'He had been sitting at Eddie's bedside and went out to learn the score,' he wrote. 'It was a shock to hear what had happened and he hurried back to the hospital where Paynter lay in a fever. Eddie was amazed, too, and insisted on getting up. They got him dressed and Voce rushed him to the ground in a car.'

Next day the nurses at the hospital got Eddie out of his bed and prepared him for the Gabba again. He and Hedley Verity (23 not out) added a vital 92 runs before Paynter finally skied a ball and was out for 83. It was quite like old times when the Australian team and the crowd gave generous applause to the little 'un as he made his way off the field back to his hospital bed. England finished with a score of 356, just 16 runs ahead of Australia.

Australia collapsed in their second innings for 175 runs, leaving England only 163 to win the match and the Ashes. I could not help smiling to myself when Bradman was given the ball to bowl, with Hammond at the crease. Believe it or not, Bradman's first ball was a full toss, deliberate or accidental I wouldn't know. Hammond had bitter memories of Adelaide (and so did I) and he treated the ball as if it were a live bomb, gently patting it back to the grinning bowler.

On the fifth day, England went after the required 163 runs at a funereal pace, losing Sutcliffe for only two runs. Jardine hung around for 132 minutes in making only 24, thus resurrecting the ire of the crowd, while Maurice Leyland pushed the score along with a sterling 86. They crawled along and at stumps only 53 runs were needed for victory.

Australian had more to mourn on the last day than the loss of the Ashes. The flags were at half-mast at the Gabba and the Australians wore black armlets as they came out to field. A.A. (Archie) Jackson had died early that morning of tuberculosis at the age of only twenty-three in a Brisbane hospital and the whole cricket world mourned his premature passing. Just after midnight he had asked for the Test score and died shortly afterwards. Johnny Moyes reflected the opinion of most cricket followers when he wrote, 'Had Archie lived he would have been one of the master batsmen of all time'.

A tall, slight, fair-haired boy, with an engaging and modest personality, Jackson was playing for New South Wales at the age of seventeen. Born in Rutherglen, Scotland, he had come out to Sydney with his parents as a child. At nineteen, he became the youngest batsman in history to hit a century in his first Test against England. Jackson batted with rare artistry and grace and much courage, when required. Moyes described his batting as having a sort of 'radiance'. Jackson's body was taken from Brisbane to his home town of Sydney for burial on the same train that carried members of the Australian team for the fifth Test.

It took the English batsmen only 75 minutes to score the 53 runs for victory. Eddie Paynter had been discharged from hospital and it was wonderfully appropriate that he should be the batsman to hit the Ashes-winning run. He got hold of a loose ball from McCabe and hooked it high over square leg and the Gabba fence. It has become a famous six in cricket history and Paynter dearly wanted to take the ball back to Oswaldtwistle with him as a souvenir. A spectator had grabbed the ball but Paynter sought him out and did a deal with him—the ball for a bat and the bargain was struck. I suppose it is still in Oswaldtwistle somewhere.

So it was that England won the Ashes with six wickets in hand. The two teams toasted each other in champagne after the match as tradition demanded, but I doubt if there was much genuine warmth on the occasion. The congratulatory messages poured in, including one from King George V. It was a famous English victory, followed that night by a spirited celebratory dinner-dance at the Bellevue Hotel, with the bouncing Maguire girls in great demand.

While Eddie Paynter was being feted as a great popular 'hero' (how that word is misused!) there was another who deserved some accolades. Bowling in searing heat on an unresponsive wicket, Harold Larwood had taken 4 for 101 in the first innings and 3 for 49 in the second.

That 4 for 101 does not sound over-impressive, but during it he clean bowled Bradman and Ponsford in three overs when the score was 3 for 251 and Australian looking very dangerous indeed. It was one of his finest performances and Arthur Mailey, the great Australian googly bowler, wrote afterwards: 'I cannot remember a bowler who had a greater influence on his opponents than Larwood. The fact that he was in the field was sufficient to cause a certain amount of uneasiness in the Australian ranks. I regard him as the world's greatest bowler.'

I was curiously detached by the result. As a cuckoo or a mole in the nest, I felt neither jubilation for England nor sorrow for Australia. Although it had been an exciting and personally successful journalistic experience, I felt a sense of relief that it was nearly over. There were left only a match against New South Wales Northern Districts at Newcastle, the fifth Test in Sydney, then against South Australia at Adelaide, and a concluding game against Victoria in Melbourne.

I grieved for cricket. Regardless of the rights and wrongs of bodyline bowling, the tour had broken old friendships on and off the field and, on a wider scale, created much ill-feeling between the governments and peoples of Australia and England. Jack Fingleton was to write: 'By the end of the season the nerves of all the Australian batsmen had worn thin. I do not think there was one single batsman who played in most of those bodyline games who ever afterwards recaptured his love for cricket.'

I reflected it was just as well that the Ashes had been decided in Brisbane; a deciding Test in Sydney could develop into an Adelaide-style donnybrook with the volatile crowds on The Hill in full cry.

As the band blared out the popular dance tunes of the 1930s at the Bellevue Hotel that victory night, I sought out Plum Warner to communicate my feelings privately to him. I knew how he felt. When Eddie Paynter executed his historic six to win the Ashes, Mr Warner had exclaimed fervently, 'Now thank we all our God!'—and I understood perfectly his relief that it was all over bar the shouting, which was now taking place.

Warner had had a wretched tour, constantly reminded of his public strictures on fast leg theory bowling before the tour began. He looked worn, tired and disillusioned. His cherished 'it isn't cricket' ideals had been shattered, in his eyes. His influence on Jardine was negligible and he was weak and vacillating under pressure. He ran for cover with his stock phrases, 'I learnt at the Foreign Office never to interfere with the internal affairs of another country' and 'Like Bismarck, I can be silent in seven languages'.

I was sorry for him; he had treated me with the utmost courtesy and given me much help throughout the tour. On the other hand, treasurer Richard Palairet had not changed at all. He was thriving and catching plenty of fish in his spare time. A Jardine man to his batting pad straps, he revelled in the large amounts of money he was garnering for the MCC. The more the riots and unpleasantness, the more the money. I confided in Warner that night over a number of drinks and he recognised a fellow lover of cricket and what it had stood for.

Despite the fact that the battle for the Ashes was over, 136,790 people turned up to see the five days of the fifth Test in Sydney. England won it handsomely by eight wickets, thus winning the rubber four to one. It was full of the usual and unusual incidents, which kept me and Blue Greatorex busy with the cable men.

Australia had included in its team the burly Victorian fast bowler Harold (Bull) Alexander. He was billed as 'Australia's answer to Larwood', but he proved to be nothing more than a question-mark. He was a bit unlucky at times because of Woodfull's refusal to give him a strong leg field. In the two innings, the Bull pounded them down for 116 overs, taking one wicket for 154 runs (Verity caught behind by Oldfield for four).

Woodfull was steadfast in his refusal to resort to retaliatory measures against bodyline. Some Australian players, especially vice-captain Vic Richardson, were in favour of a counterattack but Woodfull would have none of it. 'We will play cricket in the manner in which we think it should be played,' he said, reiterating his outburst to Warner and Palairet in Adelaide. I have a feeling that he might also have decided in his own mind that Australia did not have the bowlers to succeed against the strong English batting side. Tim Wall, Bull Alexander and Laurie Nash, of Tasmania, were aggressive fast men but they were not Larwoods by any stretch of the imagination.

Bull was in the limelight for other reasons in the fifth Test.

The barrackers were out in full force to farewell Jardine from Sydney, with animosity and hostility. There was an eruption of jeers and taunts when he complained that Alexander's run-through was damaging the wicket. This turned to sustained cheering when a ball from the Bull dealt Jardine a sickening blow on the hip (his trousers were soaked in blood when he returned to the dressing room). It was not a very edifying spectacle.

On the fourth day Harold Larwood was to meet with triumph and disaster. Sent in as nightwatchman during the last over the evening before, he went on to make a rousing 98, after which the crowd gave him one of the biggest standing ovations ever heard on Sydney Cricket Ground. The irony was that he was caught out by Victorian bowler Bert (Dainty) Ironmonger, whose daintiness was a satirical reference to his butter-fingers. The crowd probably booed him for holding the catch and robbing Larwood on his first Test century but I'm not sure whether that happened.

Larwood gives generous acknowledgment of his reception in his book:

> Every man on Sydney Cricket Ground stood and cheered me. The applause and the cheers from the mob on the Hill were thunderous. I never realised the approach of Australian crowds until that moment. It proved to me Australians like a trier, they go for the underdog, and they appreciate good cricket no matter who provides it. They are tough; they barrack to unsettle a player but they like anyone who attacks. I never expected the Hill mob to get up and cheer me after the abuse they hurled.

The disaster struck Larwood later that day after Australia went in to bat. After more than four months of thumping his left leg down in his delivery stride on the hard Australian wickets, his foot finally paid the penalty. Jardine had shown little mercy to his No. 1 strike weapon and crowd-puller, appealing always for a last-ditch effort for England. Larwood had always responded to his limit until his brief rebellion at Bendigo.

Now, here in Sydney, he was again being asked for a superhuman effort to break a dangerous Bradman–Woodfull partnership, despite appeals for a spell. After the first ball of his eleventh over, he felt something go in his left foot and pulled up in sudden pain. He describes what happened next:

> Jardine came across to me and asked, 'What's wrong, Harold?'
>
> 'I've done something to my foot, Skipper, I can't walk. I think I've broken a bone.'
>
> 'You'll have to walk. You'll have to finish the over.'
>
> I began to get angry. 'I can't.'
>
> 'You'll have to.'
>
> I had five balls to go to finish the over... All I could do was stand against the crease and swing my arm over. 'Here's five fours,' I murmured to myself.
>
> Bill Woodfull patted the balls back to me. He knew I was hurt. It was the kind of sportsman he was...

Jardine refused to allow Larwood to leave the field until Bradman was bowled by Verity for 71. Then he hobbled off for an examination of his foot which was black from heel to toe. It was subsequently diagnosed as damage to the left big toe joint and the fracture of two small bones beneath the toe. Told he would never bowl again without an operation, he took no further part in the tour, postponing the operation until his return to England.

It was the last time Harold Larwood would ever bowl in a Test match. Ray Robinson was to write, 'Larwood died with his boots on'.

11

The Post Mortems

We filed aboard the steamer *Maunganui* at Sydney like a party of transported convicts for New Zealand, where two Test matches and a game against Wellington were to be played. Nobody from Australian cricket officialdom and not one member of the Australian team saw us off.

Warner had said 'Now thank we all our God!' after the Ashes were won and now we all echoed his words. We were all glad it was over. And that included me. We had travelled about 40,000 miles, spent 63 days and nights in ships, 21 nights in train sleeping cars and visited 30 different cities in five different countries.

For those interested in cricket statistics, Woodfull won the toss in four Test matches, Jardine in one. England scored 2,276 runs for 76 wickets, averaging 35.86; Australia 2,490 for 98 wickets, averaging 25.15. Paynter topped the English Test batting averages with 61.53 in 5 innings for a total of 184 runs; Bradman topped the Australian Test averages with 56.57 in 8 innings for 396 runs. Six-ball overs were bowled in Tests, eight balls in all other matches. Attendances for the five Tests totalled 759,957 with gate receipts of £70,000. Gate money for all first-class matches exceeded £90,000, a large sum of money in those days and amazing considering the country was in the depths of the Great Depression. Of that total, the MCC received nearly £40,000 in Australian currency. No wonder Mr Palairet was smiling like a Cheshire cat with a big bowl of cream.

New Zealanders gave us a rapturous welcome. There has always been intense rivalry between New Zealand and big brother Australia. The New Zealanders were jubilant that the Aussies had been humiliated, the more bodyline the better, in their opinion. The no-bodyline, no-barracking and general peace and quiet of New Zealand was difficult to cope with at first but we gradually learnt to relax and sleep well at night.

The highlight of the cricket was Wally Hammond's 336 not out against New Zealand, breaking Don Bradman's 334 record against England in 1930. It nearly did not happen. Whether it was the traditional Midlander caution of Captain Bob Wyatt (Jardine had gone fishing) or whether I had told him about my catastrophe at Colombo, I don't know. Wyatt had decided to declare the innings closed as soon as Hammond broke the record and kept a careful watch on the scoreboard. When it posted Hammond at 335 something made him check the score with Bill Ferguson. It was just as well he did—the scoreboard was one ahead of the scorebook. The declaration was delayed and another catastrophe averted.

On the way home through Canada, I wrote the first few chapters of a book about my views on the tour. In a cabin close by, Bruce Harris was also busy writing *Jardine Justified*, a book to carry a foreword by Douglas Jardine. Our views were very different, although we had established a close personal friendship which continued when we toured Australia together again with Gubby Allen's team in 1936–37.

Douglas Jardine remained as remote as ever towards me on the way back to England. One of my last memories of this extraordinary man concerned an incident in the liner *Aorangi* which took us across the Pacific to Vancouver. We had on board the English actress, Violet Vanburgh, who was returning home after a successful tour of Australia and New Zealand. With her sister, Irene, they were the two most distinguished leading ladies of the contemporary British stage. Violet graciously agreed to give a reading at the ship's concert and it was eagerly awaited by the passengers.

Now, every evening after dinner Jardine was in the habit of reading a book in a certain seat near the centre of the ship's saloon, where the concert was to be held. On this evening he took up his customary seat there and read his book through the concert, not bothering to listen to or applaud Violet Vanburgh's magnificent performance. For a Wykehamist (ex-Winchester College man) whose school motto is 'Manners Maketh Man', I thought it was an insulting public exhibition of rudeness and it did not pass unnoticed by Miss Vanburgh and the other passengers. A Jekyll and Hyde was the only way to describe him.

Team members were greeted like conquering heroes on their return to Britain but the euphoria did not last. Disturbing new aspects of the tour began to circulate. We went our separate ways and nearly all of us were to be affected in one way or another by the bodyline tour.

I reported back to Mr Rickatson-Hatt at Reuters at Blackfriars, modestly acknowledging congratulations for a job well done, or words to that effect. I obtained an audience with Sir Roderick Jones to seek permission to write my book. He asked me whose side I was on, and when I told him I was strongly opposed to bodyline, he said he thought it would be better if I did not go on with it. Understandably, I suppose, he did not want Reuters to become embroiled in controversy. So it has taken me nearly sixty years to finish the book I began in 1933.

Other members of our party suffered no such restrictions and suddenly began to speak out against bodyline, though they had been quiet enough about it when dishing it out to Australian batsmen.

I had been effectively muzzled as a journalist, but Jack Hobbs came out in the open:

I considered it bowling the purpose of which was to intimidate the batsman. In my cabled accounts of the play in Australia which appeared in the *Star*, I made no mention of my views on leg theory-cum-bodyline bowling. I purposely avoided this, because I did not wish to embarrass Jardine or his men by giving the Australians another peg on which to hang their fierce attack.

Wally Hammond, who had kept quiet about it like the rest of us, was particularly scathing on his return home. 'I condemn it absolutely,' he wrote:

> Bodyline is dangerous. I believe only good luck was responsible for the fact that no one was killed by bodyline. I have had to face it and I would have got out of the game if it had been allowed to persist. I doubt if there was any answer to such bowling unless grave risks of injury were courted.

Books and articles galore have been written about the aftermath of the bodyline affair and the eventual banning of 'direct action' bowling, interpret that euphemism for bodyline as you may. No doubt there were all kinds of questionable behind-scenes negotiations, deals and cover-ups while the MCC was considering ways and means to extricate themselves from the crisis and preserve international cricket. Certain people and players who might have rocked the boat were not called upon to give their side of the story.

The argument among players was virtually a bowlers versus batsmen affair. Very few English batsmen wanted to be in the firing line. There were some supporters of bodyline in Australia as well as England. Arthur Mailey accepted it to some extent but as far as I could tell, the overwhelming majority of players and spectators wanted an end to it. The game was too great to be destroyed if it generated such ill-feeling.

One of the main arguments of the apologists for bodyline was that English batsmen had faced similar assaults from Australia's demon bowlers of the 1920s, E.A. (Ted) McDonald and Jack Gregory. This was immediately refuted by McDonald:

I am decidedly against bodyline bowling and if Gregory and I were over there now bowling as fast as we did in 1921 we would soon stop it. My method would be retaliation. If they hurt one of our players I should do likewise, or even go one better; at any rate I should try, because I believe this type of bowling is unsportsmanlike, is reducing Test cricket to a farce, and may even spoil our great game altogether. Gregory and I were straight-up-and-downers. No matter how we were hit we never tried to bowl at the body.

Another famous English bowler did not agree with it, as mentioned earlier in this book. Ironically, F.R. Foster's captain when he skittled Australians with leg theory in 1911–12 was none other than Pelham (Plum) Warner.

'Before Jardine left England he came frequently to my flat at St James and secured from me my leg theory field placings,' Foster wrote. 'I had no hint that these would be used for bodyline bowling. I would like all my old friends in Australian cricket to know that I am sorry my experience and views were put to such unworthy uses.'

Ultimately, in 1934, the MCC passed legislation outlawing 'direct action' bowling. So another euphemism was created, but it was the word 'bodyline' that made its way into the English, and some foreign dictionaries of today. There have been some fiery bouncer wars since, but bodyline bowling of the type seen in 1932–33 has never resurfaced. The ban on 'direct action' was later adopted by the Imperial Cricket Conference.

It seems to me that Don Bradman made one of the most telling comments on the affair. 'I want to establish the all-important point that Australia did not stop bodyline bowling,' he wrote. 'Immediately the MCC committee was satisfied that such a style of bowling existed, they acted promptly and firmly to define it, and to outline the procedures to be adopted by the umpires to stop it.'

Any doubts about what James Southerton might have done had he been in my place on the tour seem to have been dispelled after he became editor of *Wisden*. He wrote a trenchant indictment of it in the 1934 edition of *Wisden Cricketers' Almanack*, ending with:

> For myself I hope we shall never see fast leg-theory bowling as used during the last tour of Australia exploited in this country. I think that (1) it is definitely dangerous (2) it creates ill-feeling between the rival teams (3) it invites reprisals (4) it has a bad influence on our great game of cricket and (5) it eliminates practically all the best strokes in batting. Mainly because it makes cricket a battle instead of a game, I deplore its introduction and pray for its abolition.

Those were my sentiments, too, but I was prevented from expressing them publicly. I still hold the opinion that the harm bodyline would have done to cricket overrode all other considerations.

Harold Larwood appeared to have been made the chief scapegoat for the affair in England. His version of the aftermath is told with bitterness and much detail in the Larwood–Kevin Perkins book. He said he was asked by the MCC to apologise for his bowling—and refused. I wonder if his Svengali, Douglas Jardine, had been asked the same question, what his response would have been?

Larwood resumed county cricket about a year after an operation on his left foot but never really regained his devastating form. He retired in 1938 to his poultry farm at the Nottinghamshire village of Angsley Woodhouse. He was the finest fast bowler I have ever seen and I agree with Johnny Moyes who wrote, 'his talents were misdirected and he dropped out of the game far too soon'.

'I have never bowled to injure a man in my life,' Larwood said in his book. 'Frighten them, intimidate them, yes.' Kevin Perkins, his literary collaborator, wrote:

> He soon dropped out of the game, disillusioned with his treatment at the hands of the Establishment which exploited

his rare talent so exhaustively, then tried to make a scapegoat of him. Later he migrated with his family to Australia, where he thought some hatred might linger towards him still. But instead, he found happiness and contentment—and a host of friends.

It was many years before the story was revealed of the Anglo-Australian political and diplomatic intrigue and manoeuvring that went on behind the scenes during the bodyline tour. Some facts are still believed to be hidden in files in London and Canberra, others have been 'accidentally' destroyed. I commend *Cricket and Empire*, by Ric Sissons and Brian Stoddart, published in 1984 as the most thoughtful and best researched book on the subject.

The book emphasised the social and political context of the bodyline tour and the fact that, for the first time, politics were publicly seen as part of sport. 'In the course of two weeks [at Adelaide] the relatively simple fact of two Australian batsmen being struck by an English bowler had grown into a major imperial problem at the highest political levels,' the authors wrote. 'While those most directly involved, the cricketers, became almost secondary players, the ramifications became increasingly complex.'

The main political and diplomatic players included the prime minister of Australia, J.A. (Joe) Lyons, the British secretary of state for the dominions, J.H. (Jimmy) Thomas, Robert Gordon Menzies, the British representative in Canberra, Ernest Crutchley, and the governor of South Australia, Sir Alexander Hore-Ruthven (afterwards governor-general of Australia as Lord Gowrie).

Co-author of *Cricket and Empire* Brian Stoddart was a professional Australian historian who in 1977 received a small government grant to probe into the bodyline affair and the role of sport in modern society, especially the delicate matter of sport and politics. There was some criticism of the grant. A prominent Australian columnist wrote, 'Lord only knows what's left to research about bodyline. No controversy in sporting history has been so exhaustively covered, so remorselessly analysed, so boringly discussed and so endlessly written about.'

Well, in 1992, the interest in it is as keen as ever and there is still plenty more to write about it. Stoddart spent more than five years on the job and dug up a lot of new material.

His co-author, Ric Sissons, was a bright young English writer who came to Australia on a two-year assignment for celebrated British film producer, David Puttnam, who was planning a major film on bodyline, to be directed by Bruce Beresford, with Ben Cross in the part of Douglas Jardine. Puttnam had won a Hollywood Oscar for his *Chariots of Fire*, with Cross as the Olympic Games Jewish runner, Harold Abrahams.

Ric Sissons flew from Sydney to my home in Port Macquarie in October 1983, to quiz me about the bodyline tour for the book and Puttnam's film. He had already been given access to the Australian Cricket Board's bodyline file but told me that a file of letters from Sir Alexander Hore-Ruthven was still being kept secret at Lord's by the MCC. Hore-Ruthven, then governor of South Australia in Adelaide, the seat of the bodyline explosion, wrote letters to the British government and the MCC stating that the facts of the bodyline case had never been fairly presented and that the strong anti-Australian feeling in England was, in many ways, unjustified.

Ric said the index of a Dominions Office file on bodyline had been recently discovered in Whitehall, but the documents themselves had been accidentally destroyed. Other documents had been destroyed during World War II, but a telegram from Australian Prime Minister Lyons expressing concern about the effects of the bodyline crisis on a loan being negotiated with Britain had been unearthed.

'Jimmy' Thomas is quoted as saying in a speech:

> My job as Dominions secretary is to reconcile the different
> elements in the British Commonwealth. When you remember
> that that includes South Africa, Canada, Australia, New
> Zealand and the Irish Free State, they take some managing
> don't they? No politics ever introduced in the British Empire
> caused me so much trouble as this damn bodyline bowling!

The Sissons-Stoddart book closely examines the wider
implications of the bodyline affair, with penetrating pen-
pictures of the leading characters in the drama. 'The tour
remains a major benchmark in the evolution of Anglo-
Australian imperial and social attitudes,' the authors
conclude.

Sad to say, Puttnam's bodyline film has never been made
for reasons not known to me. In its place we were given an
Australian-made TV mini-series in 1984. It was a huge
popular success, but it was spoilt for me because it was wrong
in too many places. Maybe my criticisms will sound trivial
but it is a pity that stories like this, purporting to be factual,
are not researched properly.

As noted earlier, the RMS *Orontes* left Tilbury with two
funnels and arrived in Fremantle with three. The amateurs
were shown in dinner jackets on the ship at night, the
professionals in day suits. We all wore dinner jackets.

Bradman was shown in the Members Stand at Sydney
Cricket Ground watching the first Test. He was ill at home.
There were women in the stand, too, and that was strictly
taboo in those days.

The second Test at Melbourne had Bradman walking back
to the pavilion after his first-ball duck like a gloomy head-
shrunken Hamlet. In fact, he went back with his head in
the air and the familiar wide boyish grin on his face, which
boded no good for the English bowlers in the second innings.

(It reminded me at the time of a remark by Neville Cardus

when Bradman was on his run-spree in 1930, 'Perhaps by making a duck some day, Bradman will oblige some of his critics who believe with Lord Bacon that there should always be some strangeness, something unexpected, mingled with art and beauty'.)

When Bradman duly got his century in the second innings, we were shown a ludicrous scene of 60,000 spectators singing 'Our Don Bradman'. I doubt if many of them knew the song, let alone the words.

Bradman with a half-finished glass of beer in his hand also startled me—he never touched the stuff.

The most grotesque caricature was the portrayal of Pelham (Plum) Warner, granted that he was very weak in his handling of Jardine. A charming and polished Englishman, Warner was turned into a half-drunken scowling introvert.

A Union Jack was not burned on top of the Adelaide Oval grandstand and Jardine did not knock on the players' hotel bedroom doors at night to seek a vote of confidence in the bar downstairs. The meeting was called by Herbert Sutcliffe in a room upstairs and Jardine was invited in afterwards.

And now to a personal note. During the run of the TV series in Sydney I received unwanted mention in Column 8 on the front page of the *Sydney Morning Herald*:

> Viewers of the *Bodyline* TV series may have noticed a faintly raffish character in a hat around the English cricketers' dressing room. Tom Goodman, the *Herald*'s tour correspondent who has been watching the series, says, this character was not an Australian but an English pressman from the Reuters agency, Gilbert Mant, who covered the tour for the English dailies. Tom recalls that the English captain, Jardine, clashed with Mant over his stories about the bodyline attack. The Reuters reporter now lives in retirement on the N.S.W. Mid-North Coast.

This, of course, was nonsense and a practical joke on me by Tom Goodman. The word 'raffish' disturbed me as the dictionary defines it as 'disreputable, dissipated, tawdry' and some of my associates referred to me at the time as DDT.

The raffish character in the series was an ocker caricature of an Australian newspaperman. Although most journalists in those days were impecunious, the scene where he coined the word 'bodyline' through lack of money for a telegram was fiction of the highest and most ridiculous order.

Maybe it was this mini-series that influenced David Puttnam to abandon his film project. The story is still here waiting to be told in a *Chariots of Fire* manner. Over to you, David Puttnam.

12
Close of Innings

All that was sixty years ago and there are now few survivors of that 'damn bodyline bowling' business Jimmy Thomas spoke about. 'During the year after the tour the Establishment quietly changed the fast-bowling rules, to save lives, though it never accepted responsibility for what it had permitted to happen,' Alistair Mant wrote in his book, *Leaders We Deserve*.

The wounds were healed, the bonds of Empire restored. Normal cricket resumed for the next forty years or so when another crisis occurred. Australian media magnate, Mr Kerry Packer, started purchasing national cricket teams for commercial one-day contests, a development that may yet result in the death of traditional Test cricket as we knew it. Its demise was predicted in the London *Times* in May 1977, by three journalists travelling with the touring Australian team: 'In affectionate remembrance of International Cricket which died in Hove, 9th May, 1977. Deeply lamented by a large circle of friends and acquaintances. R.I.P. N.B.—The body will be cremated and the Ashes taken to Australia and scattered around the studios of TCN9 in Sydney. NTJCBM.'

This, of course, parodied a notice in *The Times* when Australia defeated England in 1882: 'In affectionate remembrance of English cricket which died at the Oval on 29th August 1882. Deeply lamented by a large circle of sorrowing friends and acquaintances. R.I.P. N.B.—The body will be created and the Ashes taken to Australia.' The Ashes have remained the symbol of cricket supremacy between England and Australia ever since.

Plum Warner became Sir Pelham in 1937, president of the MCC and had a grandstand named after him at Lord's, the agonies of the bodyline tour gradually receding like a bad dream. Mr Palairet, I presume, retired and went fishing.

Douglas Jardine was dropped by the cricket Establishment as soon as it decently could and he slipped into public obscurity. He married Irene Margaret Peat, daughter of Sir Harry Peat, a prominent accountant, in 1934. They spent their honeymoon big game hunting in East Africa, both of them being good shots. It was said that he always stalked a wounded animal himself on the principle 'Fear and be slain'. Despite his dislike of journalists, he became a part-time one himself, writing cricket for the London *Daily Telegraph*.

Jardine served with distinction in World War II; nobody had ever doubted his courage and fortitude. He went to France with the British Expeditionary Force in 1940 as an officer in the Royal Berkshire Regiment and was caught up in the Dunkirk evacuation. He served later in India, where he became fluent in Hindustani and engrossed in Eastern mysticism.

After the war he again turned to cricket commentary for the London *Star* and radio. He visited Australia in the early 1950s, being chairman of the N.S.W. Land Agency Company and on the board of the Scottish Australian Company. There were no demonstrations against him. It was all too long ago, although he is still regarded in Australia as the villain of the bodyline piece and a symbol of the English old-school-tie establishment. A strange sidelight is that although the name of Jardine was reviled in the southern States of Australia during the 'trouble', it was still revered in far north Queensland. Captain John Jardine and his three sons were pioneers of Cape York Peninsula at the northernmost tip of Australia in the 1860s. One son, the flamboyant Frank Jardine, who married a beautiful Samoan princess, is a legend of the Top End. The Jardines were direct descendants of a Scottish baronetcy created in 1672 in Dumfriesshire. Douglas Jardine was said to have been a distant cousin and this seems reinforced by the nature of the family coat of arms. It is supported by a horse rampant and a man in armour and the motto is, 'Beware, I am present!'

According to Sissons and Stoddart, Jardine retained his interest in psychic matters and Hinduism, developing an antipathy to Christianity. He was excited by discussion of ethics and religion.

In 1957, Douglas Jardine travelled to Rhodesia to inspect land he owned and developed tick fever. Tests in England revealed an advanced stage of cancer and he died in a Swiss sanitorium in 1958 at the age of fifty-eight. He left a widow, three daughters and a son. His ashes were scattered over the top of Cross Craigs mountain in Perthshire, Scotland. He had been a great family man and they had adored him. Christopher Douglas, his biographer, wrote, 'His wife, in a state of abject grief, destroyed all his cricket clothes and equipment.'

I still regret that Jardine was so unbending towards me; we might even have become friends. Bill O'Reilly has told how he got to know Jardine in later tours of England as a cricketer and writer. 'I drank champagne with him from a pewter pot in the rooms of the Master of Trinity at Oxford in 1948,' he wrote. 'We sank the bubbly as well as the hatchet.' I'm sorry to this day that Jardine and I could not have buried the hatchet over a pewter pot of champagne, as well.

Neville Cardus wrote of him:

Jardine will go down in the history of the game as one of the strongest and sternest and most realistic of all English captains. He has no moonshine in his make-up; he is a Scot, and in the habit of counting the change given him in any match... He has remained master of himself against all the roaring of The Hill at Sydney; I have indeed felt sorry for the Hill, pour souls, with their howls and contumely, splitting the heavens in vain while Jardine has gone his way ruthlessly... I admire Jardine beyond words but I dislike his view of cricket. I believe that the qualities of character he possesses would suit better a leader of armies than a leader of cricketers.

What of Don Bradman, the catalyst of the whole affair? He did not fail and was only temporarily tamed, as his Test batting average of 56.57 testified. Some criticised his method of combating bodyline by stepping away to cut the ball to the off, but Bradman claimed that this exposed him to a greater risk of injury than the orthodox type of batting. He had some strong and influential defenders.

Here's Neville Cardus again, paying tribute to Bradman drawing across to the on-side and, having made the pitch of the ball fall on the off-side, cracking it through the covers:

> Astounding and audacious! Desperate maybe, but what else could have been done in the circumstances? Bradman's measures against fast leg-side attack were severely censured by several of his playing contemporaries. Their main argument was that his improvisations suggested no long tenure at the crease and were therefore likely to disturb the less-gifted colleagues, waiting and watching while the moth darted in and out of the flame.
>
> But there was no rational means of 'digging in', or of planning a long, deliberately executed innings against Larwood and the leg-field. The situation called for nerve and originality. In all his career, Bradman did little that was more wonderful and so highly charged with his own force of character than his dazzling improvisation, his neck-to-nothing brilliance, in the face of the ruthless challenge of Jardine thrown down in 1932–33.

Bradman himself devotes only fourteen pages to the bodyline tour in his *Farewell to Cricket*, published after his retirement in 1950. 'The last thing I want to do at the close of my career is to revive unpleasant memories,' he wrote. However, his description of a batsman's dilemma in facing bodyline needs to be recorded:

> A batsman who played defensively would certainly get caught by one of the short-leg fieldsmen. To try to hook the ball would result sooner or later in a catch to the boundary. Neither defence nor attack could overcome it for long, unless the batsman was particularly lucky. Playing the good length balls and dodging the others may sound all right in theory, but it would not work in practice. The batsman doing this must of necessity be hit.

Bradman resumed his amazing career, breaking record after record, until stumps were drawn at the outbreak of World War II in 1939 for six years. He had scored 758 runs at an average of 94.75 in the 1934 tour of England.

This is not a book about Don Bradman but it may be appropriate to reprint a piece I wrote about him when I was a columnist on the Sydney *Sunday Sun* (now defunct) in 1946. He had accepted the captaincy of Australia against the first postwar MCC touring team on the resumption of international cricket:

> Being a national hero in Australia—or anywhere else—isn't much fun. Kingsford Smith found that out.
>
> Bernborough [a racehorse] and Bradman will find it out someday, too—if they haven't found it out already.
>
> You're still a national hero when the whole nation avidly reads, day by day, conflicting reports about your health, and when a newspaper devotes the entire billboard to the words 'BRADMAN FAILS'—as happened in Sydney this week.
>
> One cross a national hero has to bear is to have things

written about him, such as I am writing now. The thing to do is bear it and grin. Don Bradman has a rather infectious grin.

But he has his detractors, as all national heroes have.

Much of it is of a petty nature, and springs from jealousy, but at times I have heard the most outrageous things said about him.

The trouble with being a national hero is that, to please some people, you would have to be a ludicrous cross between a Sir Galahad, a spendthrift, a congenital drunkard and a selfless monk.

Bradman is none of these things.

The worst crime he has committed in the eyes of some people, is to have looked after himself and become steeped in suburban respectability as a devoted family man. The world today could do with a bit more suburban respectability of this kind.

Bradman has been attacked for 'running away from bodyline'. It's much more important, I think, to remember that he enlisted in the Royal Australian Air Force in 1940.

The way I see it, I'm watching with a great deal of admiration Bradman's fight to come back into big cricket.

He turned down two fat English newspaper contracts to do it. I cannot believe, as it has been suggested to me, that he is doing it just because big cricket will help his stockbroking business in Adelaide.

Cricket made Bradman and I prefer to believe that he wants to give to Australian cricket what it gave to him.

He has been dogged by bad luck in recent years. The Hodgetts stockbroking crash came as a shock. And there have been recurrent illnesses and family tragedy.

I hope he makes a triumphant comeback. For what I've always liked best about Don Bradman during an acquaintanceship of many years is his disarming personal modesty.

That's a rare thing with national heroes (Smithy had it, too) and rarer still with international sportsmen.

The Don (the great Charles Fry conferred the title on him) made a triumphant comeback, captaining the champion 1948 Australian side that came back from England undefeated. He became Sir Donald Bradman in 1949 and later a Companion of the Order of Australia. Grandstands and ovals were named after him and he became chairman of the Australian Cricket Board of Control, with which he had had so many quarrels in the past.

It was a pity that he was subject at times to small-minded personal criticism, particularly from Jack Fingleton, his former Test colleague. Fingleton, who played in three Tests of the series and finished with a 'pair', chose 1946–47, the year of Bradman's comeback, to write on bodyline. A.G. (Johnny) Moyes, in his biography of Bradman, criticised Fingleton for his remarks about Bradman's part in the affair:

> He seemed to suggest that the great batsman placed his own skin before the interests of the side while others gallantly took all the knocks. Woodfull, he said, ordered his bowlers to give away their wickets rather than be hit. This did not apply to batsmen, who were, one supposes, to be hit, and perhaps injured in Australia's cause. I thought that Jack's comments were far below the standard of his returns from cover point and not nearly as convincing. Each batsman had a problem to solve. He had to solve it according to his own ability and conception of his power of batsmanship. . . There was no real solution. Bradman at least went on making runs. His critics did not.

I, too, thought that Fingleton's continued personal vendetta against Bradman was out of order and marred his otherwise excellent books on cricket. I told him so on the few occasions we met after the war, but he did not reply. I can only say that my meetings with Don Bradman, as a journalist and on a personal level, are occasions I look back on with pleasure and gratitude for help given to me in my work. My admiration for him as a cricketer and a man is boundless.

These mischievous attacks hurt Bradman enough for him to refer to them in his *Farewell to Cricket*:

> it would be incorrect for me to say that I did not at times notice a particularly vicious and persistent criticism from certain quarters—the type of comment which is based on facts but obviously of the kind which is inspired by an innermost desire to find fault whether it exists or not...
>
> At times jealousy can become an obsession and assume the character of positive hatred until the accuser reveals it so unmistakeably that he becomes an object of pity. The flame he so carefully fans into a fire consumes him. The object of his wrath becomes undisturbed.

Today, the national hero has grown into an enduring bona fide Australian folk hero with such unlikely companions as Sydney Harbour Bridge, Ned Kelly (a bushranger, or highwayman), Phar Lap (a racehorse) and Les Darcy (a boxer). There's nothing Sir Donald can do about it and he accepts it with dignity and a grin.

And me? Sir Roderick Jones took away with one hand but gave with another. In 1934 I was promoted to become Reuters News Editor for Canada, with headquarters in Ottawa. Then, in 1936, I was withdrawn to be the Reuter-PA correspondent with the 1936–37 MCC tour of Australia under the captaincy of my old next-door-neighbour, Gubby Allen.

There was a large contingent of press representatives this time, hoping for more sensation and violence. Alas, all was sweetness and light. The desire for reconciliation became so cloying that sometimes I yearned for the bad old days of bodyline. About the only exciting thing was the jealous and sometimes comic running feud between those two dissimilar cricket writer luminaries, Neville Cardus and C.B. (Charles) Fry.

But all that, as Rudyard Kipling used to say, is another story.

13

The Pyjama Game

The game of cricket has undergone many changes and survived a number of major crises since its inception about 800 years ago. It faces its biggest challenge today as the sport has virtually split into two different games, with two different audiences.

It is believed that the first cricket was played with a crooked stick about the year 1180. Knights of the day batted and bowled at two sticks, or wickets, with a third across the top. It was first referred to by the name of 'creckett' about 1550. The bodyline rumpus of 1932–33 was mild stuff compared to the early years of the game and fatalities were not unusual. It is not clear for what reason, but Oliver Cromwell forbade the playing of 'krickett' in Ireland in 1656 and ordered all 'sticks and balls' to be burnt by the common hangman. In 1693 spectators at a match at Lewes (England) were fined for riot and battery.

The game flourished in eighteenth-century Georgian England. It was a reckless age of violence, gambling and general profligacy. Cricketers were bribed to 'throw' matches and this resulted in wild scenes and riots at matches, with firearms being used. Duels were fought over games, with fatal results. Frederick, Prince of Wales, president of the exclusive London Club, died from an abscess caused by a blow from a cricket ball in 1751.

Cricket was gradually refined, a third stump and bails added, the rules adjusted and all firearms banned at matches. At first the sole preserve of the landed gentry and the rich, the game became a popular pastime for the masses and, in time, the national sport of England. As Plum Warner had put it, the game also became a synonym for all that was true and honest. To say that it was 'not cricket' implied something underhand not in keeping with the best ideals. This tradition, however, was not able to withstand the Age of Greed in a later century.

The Bodyline War in 1932–33 was the first serious cricket crisis of the twentieth century and we have seen how it came to a fairly satisfactory settlement. Australia stayed within the Empire with the Union Jack intact in the top left-hand corner of our flag.

The Basil D'Olivera Affair of 1968 was an England–South Africa dispute and did not affect Australia to any great extent. D'Olivera was a 'Cape coloured' South African cricketer who, under apartheid, was not allowed to play with or against white South Africans. A talented batsmen, he sought his future in England and graduated to the England Test team, playing against Australia. But when he was chosen to tour with England against South Africa, the South African cricket bosses refused to accept him. England stood firm; the tour was cancelled, as was a later tour by South Africa to England.

The bodyline and D'Olivera affairs were minor skirmishes compared with what became known as the Packer affair. President Franklin Roosevelt described 7 December 1941 as a 'day of infamy' when Japan made a devastating sneak attack on the Pearl Harbor naval base in World War II. Diehard cricket buffs still refer to 9 May 1977 as another day of infamy when Mr Kerry Packer, of Australia, announced the purchase of thirty-five of the world's leading cricketers for a series of international one-day and five-day games under the title of World Series Cricket. Most of his acquisitions signed contracts for a period of three years and for as much in some instances as $50,000 a year.

The cricket mercenaries were to be recruited from Australia, England, Pakistan, the West Indies and South

Africa. They included the South African-born captain of England, Tony Greig, who was smartly sacked by the English cricket Establishment. The Australian buys were the Australian ex-captain, Ian Chappell, the current captain, Greg Chappell, Ian Redpath, Ross Edwards, Dennis Lillee, Jeff Thomson, Ian Davis, Rick McCosker, David Hookes, Doug Walters, Rod Marsh, Richard Robinson, Kerry O'Keefe, Gary Gilmour, Max Walker, Michael Malone, Len Pascoe and Ray Bright. Their duties were to play cricket for Kerry Packer during the Australian summer, the matches to be shown on his Channel Nine Australian television network.

The announcement of the Packer coup was made without warning on 9 May at the beginning of the 1977 Australian Test tour of England. The negotiations had taken place in tight secrecy and the *fait accompli* came like a bombshell on the cricket world. Adjectives such as 'shady', 'underhand' and 'betrayal' were bandied about within the Establishment. In one fell swoop the Packer coup answered many of the questions about the future of the game posed by John Arlott, Fred Truman, Gilbert Phelps and David Frith in BBC Further Education Television programs aired only a month earlier. In a book about the programs John Arlott was saying that cricket, like a number of other sports, was not viable in itself:

It is dependent on sponsorship, publicity, and payments from the media, none of which is necessarily permanent. It is not capable, though, of continuing to exist on its national revenue from subscriptions and gate money. A by no means impossible cutback in the national economy could see the loss of sponsorship and publicity. A change in public taste to a cheaper form of entertainment could—though improbably—remove or reduce the payments from television, in which, unfortunately for cricket negotiators, there is no competition. Commercial television companies have shown clearly that they are not interested in cricket.

Well, Packer was showing clearly that his commercial television company was very interested in cricket. He was also responding in large amounts of hard cash to Arlott's lament that professional cricketers were the poor relations of the sporting world. Tennis players, golfers and footballers earned astronomically higher incomes than cricketers, Arlott said. Even a club golf pro earned a much larger income than an English county cricketer. Football League professionals were earning three times the amount of a capped county cricketer and there were 2,000 professional League footballers in England alone in 1977, compared with, at most, 180 capped county cricketers.

The rest of the story is familiar. After a shaky and controversial start, the WSC took over and became a huge popular success. The Establishment, after a flurry of indignation and mock heroics, decided that it could not beat them, so it joined them. The mercenaries were put into coloured clothes and armed with helmets and other protective gear. (England's Mike Brearley had been a helmet pioneer in traditional cricket). Night cricket came in and the red ball became white. The rules, procedures and standards were changed until it was a different game from the old game. The cricketers and the spectators spoke a new and different language. The new cricket was soon dubbed the 'pyjama game' by the traditionalists, but such ridicule had no effect on its popularity in all cricket-playing countries.

I must confess that I took it all rather badly at the outset, as shown by the following letter of mine published in the *Sydney Morning Herald* in May 1980:

The Australian cricket season over and, for me, it is the end of all cricket after a lifetime of devoted watching and playing. After 25 years, I intend to resign my membership of Sydney Cricket Ground which is good news for one of the 22,000 on the waiting list.

It saddens me to think that a noble game has been destroyed by some players bearing famous names whose betrayal was a shock to their friends and admirers. A supine Australian Cricket Board, in failing to discipline its unruly extroverts, is also responsible. I do not blame Mr Kerry Packer, who as far as I know, has no particular love for or loyalty to the game of cricket. He could just as easily have promoted tiddly-winks or darts had the opportunity been there.

Test cricket has degenerated into a greedy and insecure game with a new breed of loutish crowds. What they did to cricket was described with unintentional irony by Andrew Caro, a former WSC excecutive: 'The middle-class humbug about character-building, fair play and respectability which is summed up in the words "It's not cricket" has been exposed for what it is...and what is more, it's not promotable and it does not generate the cash'.

So for me, it's back to the 'middle-class humbug' of beloved books about cricket by J.M. Barrie, Hugh de Selincourt, Neville Cardus, John Arlott, R.C. Robertson-Glasgow, Allan Miller, A.G. Macdonell, Ray Robinson and so many others. As for the present-day fellows out in the middle well, it just isn't cricket any more.

I've mellowed a lot since then and it would be inaccurate and unfair to regard me as an old fuddy-duddy, a traditionalist muttering into my gin and tonic about 'pyjama games' and 'rock and roll cricket'. In fact, looking back, I think indignation played a lesser role in my decision to resign my membership of Sydney Cricket Ground; I had forsaken the city for the country and could not afford the high membership fees any more. The fact that I still like Test cricket does not mean that I have anything against the one-dayers. If that's what the people want today, that's what they get and good luck to them. I have learnt to live with it though I would not pay to see a one-day match. I watch it on television, enjoying the early hours but becoming frustrated and angry by the stupid run-outs and the wild cross-bat slogging by gifted batsmen in a desperate effort to beat the limited overs and the clock. It's the excitement of the slogging that the crowds have come to see. It puzzles me that the so very, very English game of cricket, even in its jazzed-up changed form, draws the crowds in our new multicultural Australian society. I would have thought that baseball, with its constant uncomplicated hitting and running, would develop into Australia's king of summer sports.

Yes, the game of cricket has changed, even the barracking. There are no more off-the-cuff Yabbas. The crowds show their displeasure with a chorus of boos at times but it is mostly done with banners and placards, some very clever and funny, others crude and pointless. My favourite was aimed in friendly fashion at young Phil Tuffnell, the English spin bowler whose clumsy and ineffectual fielding often had the crowd laughing. One day a large placard appeared on a grandstand fence directing students to The Phillip Tuffnell Academy of Fielding.

Graeme Wright, a New Zealander, made some scathing remarks about the game when he gave up his editorship of *Wisden* this year:

> There are loads of reasons for my going, but the main one is the state of the modern game. The things I value, such as sporting play, are no longer valued. Cricket has become too much of a business. The prime concern of administrators around the world is making money, not providing entertainment. Players just go through the motions and their lack of pleasure is conveyed to the crowds. Cultural rot has set in.

There is no doubt that one-day limited over cricket is here to stay. When the great Imran Khan went home to Pakistan with the 1992 World Cup in his grasp he was mobbed and worshipped like a god. He said then that the youth of Pakistan had all 'gone mad' on one-day cricket and all the kids wanted to play or watch. So popular has the game become in Imran's home town that new laws have been passed prohibiting cricket 'in thoroughfares, public streets and roads within the revenue limits of Lahore'. Offenders face up to six months in prison. The crackdown has come because windows and car windscreens are being broken and passers-by hit by balls as Pakistani children play cricket in the streets.

I'm sad, though, to think that Test cricket may not survive. There does not seem to me to be room for both games and the one-dayers will probably be changed even further in the future to hold the audiences. Test cricket will wither on the financial vine as its older supporters die out and, as Andrew Caro so bluntly put it, it doesn't generate the cash. Sydney cricket writer Brian Mossop put it sympathetically and pragmatically in a splendid article in the *Weekend Australian* this year. It sums up just about everyting I feel about the game and I have permission to reproduce parts of it here:

> Traditional cricket is in its death throes. By the turn of the century Test cricket will be but a memory, an old-fashioned game to be spoken of when those of us old enough to remember it sit around reminiscing over a glass of fine cognac—or perhaps a stubby of beer.
>
> As one devoted to Test cricket, it comes as a sad realisation that the sands of time are running out on a game which spawned an English language phrase relating to sportsmanship; a game which encouraged fine writing and some wonderfully colourful broadcasting.
>
> One-day cricket may be the money-spinner, but for the sheer exhilaration of an engaging contest there is nothing—at least not in a cricketing sense—to match the battle of wits which can develop between two keen sides, two astute captains, between bowler and batsman. But that is vanishing, giving way to the one-day game to the extent that the latter now draws from commentators—disappointingly, distressingly even—superlatives which leave you wondering about your own sense of values.

It is an old chestnut I know. But while there is a place for the one-day game which does after all give succour to cricket overall, it is so entirely different as to be a game akin to cricket yet not the same—the *Reader's Digest* version of a beautifully written novel.

Its popularity is unquestioned, coming, I am informed by a friend planted firmly on a generation behind me, from the fact that it offers a result in a day, that there is no value in waiting five days for a result which may turn out to be a draw. This is the instant generation.

The result will be the destruction of Test cricket with all of its nuances, its subtleties, its developing situations, counter moves, psychological ploys. The brash slog, it seems, is the stuff to set the blood racing. And it does, within limits, even in older veins. The trouble is the incessant demand for instant gratification. One-day cricket may have been the saviour of the game, but it is to first-class cricket what the female black widow is to the male arachnid—a predator who turns on her mate once satisfied. There is no room, it seems, for tradition; no desire to care for the history; no time to teach, or to learn, the variations applicable to the more carefully constructed game of cricket. Yet tradition, allowing that change is inevitable and necessary, is very much a part and parcel of cricket as it was.

There is a place for both games. But the more carefully crafted of the two is rapidly giving way to the quick fix. It is as much a reflection of today's attitudes as Test cricket was of its—and should still be. Times change, but not everything once held dear needs to change because of it. Adaptation is one thing. But a totally new and different approach offers a totally new and different product. The sadness is that, in cricket's case, it is happening at the expense of a product which once offered a set of sound values— values which have become as eroded as those in our daily lives. Field placings for the one-day game, batting itself— once an art—the very attack, require an approach vastly different from that taken in a Test match. Wickets mean far less than they do in a Test. Containment is the name of the game. Excitement, yes. But there is excitement, too, in Test cricket as a game unfolds. The tragedy is that without the understanding which comes from growing up with a game which has more to it than pure smash and grab, appreciation dies...

It would be nice to be wrong about where cricket is headed. It would be wonderful to be proved so.

That's exactly as I feel, too. I hope the old game survives because it has given me so many magical moments as a player and watcher. The memories of those leaving a one-day game will be of Tom Moody or Simon O'Donnell hitting gigantic sixers, but mine will be different.

I will remember the artistry and great moments of the world's most famous batsmen and bowlers. And I will remember the day at Ricksmansworth when Australia House pulled off an exciting victory over an insurance company in the natural English twilight, and the day we kept the mayor of Picton waiting on a rough Australian cricket ground.

John Arlott, who died this year, was one of my favourite writers on cricket. He wrote more than thirty books about the game, as well as other topics, and books of verse. His love of cricket came out warmly also in his BBC radio commentaries. He seemed to be taking every listener into a kind of avuncular confidence as he described, in his deep and distinctive English county accent, every facet of the play, with flashes of droll humour when required. In an introduction to one of his books, Arlott wrote this passage: ' "No he's not at home, he's gone to the cricket," my mother used to say. Now my wife uses the same words.'

It is claimed that Rugby union football is the game they play in Heaven but I like to think that when the time comes, someone will ask 'Where's Gilbert?' and someone will gently say, 'He's gone to the cricket'.

Bibliography

Arlott, John, *Gone to the Cricket*, Longmans, Green & Co., London 1948

Arlott and Truman on Cricket, edited by Gilbert Phelps, British Broadcasting Corporation, London 1977

Blofeld, Henry, *The Packer Affair*, Collins, London 1978

Bradman, Don, *Farewell to Cricket*, The Pavilion Books, London 1950

Cardus, Neville, *Good Days*, Jonathon Cape, London 1934

Douglas, Christopher, *Douglas Jardine – Spartan Cricketer*, George Allen & Unwin, London

Fingleton, J.H., *Brightly Fades the Don*, Collins, London-Sydney 1949

Fingleton, J.H., *Cricket Crisis*, Cassell & Co. Ltd, Sydney 1946

Harris, Bruce, *Jardine Justified*, Chapman and Hall, London 1933

Hele, George and R.S. Whitington, *Bodyline Umpire*, Rigby Ltd, Adelaide 1974

Jardine, Douglas, *In Quest of the Ashes*, George Allen & Unwin, London

Larwood, Harold and Kevin Perkins, *The Larwood Story*, Bonpara Pty Ltd, Sydney 1982

Luck, Peter, *This Fabulous Century*, Lansdowne Press, Sydney, 1980

Mailey, Arthur, *And Then Came Larwood*, John Lane The Bodley Head Ltd, London 1933

Mant, Alistair, *Leaders We Deserve*, Basil Blackwell, Oxford 1985

Menzies, Robert Gordon, *Afternoon Light*, Cassell, Australia 1967

Moyes, A.G., *Bradman*, Angus & Robertson, Sydney 1948

Moyes, A.G., *A Century of Cricketers*, Angus & Robertson, Sydney 1950

Pollard, Jack, *Australian Cricket*, Angus & Robertson, Sydney 1989

Robinson, Ray, *Between Wickets*, Collins, London 1946

Rundell, Michael, *The Dictionary of Cricket*, Allen & Unwin, London

Sissons, Ric and Brian Stoddart, *Cricket and Empire*, George Allen & Unwin, Sydney 1984

Swanton, E.W., *Sort of a Cricket Person*, Collins, London 1972

Swanton, E.W., *Follow On*, Collins, London 1977

Index

The Sund

and Sh

NO. 18 499   (SIXTIETH YEAR)   WEDNE

HAMMOND

Australia Falter

BRADMAN'S VAIN FIGHT WITH WOODFULL

Another "Duck" for Fingleton :: In-and-Out Ponsford

ENGLAND'S WINNING WAY

Ames and Verity piled on the agony for Australia when England resumed her second innings in the third Test match at Adelaide to-day. The Kent wicket-keeper batsman and the young Yorkshire bowler put on 98 for the seventh wicket and although the last two wickets cost Australia only 17 runs they were set the task of topping a total of 531 for victory.

The present series of Tests have been remarkable for weak send-offs, therefore it was quite in order that Australia should open in a tragic manner.

Fingleton was cleaned bowled by Larwood before opening his account, thus registering his second "duck" in this game. Another valuable wicket fell cheaply when Ponsford fell to Larwood with his total at three—then came Bradman.

Skipper Woodfull and the great Don put a different complexion on the proceedings, but Australia's star appeared to be setting when Bradman was caught and bowled by Verity with 100 runs on the board.

England are well on the road to victory.

THE SCORE BOARD

ENGLAND: 1st innings, 341.

AUSTRALIA: 1st innings, 222.

ENGLAND—2nd innings

D. R. Jardine lbw b Ironmonger...	56
Sutcliffe c sub b Wall	7
R. E. S. Wyatt c Wall b O'Reilly...	49
G. O. Allen lbw b Grimmett	15
Hammond b Bradman	85
Leyland c Wall b Ironmonger ...	42
Ames b O'Reilly	69
Verity lbw b O'Reilly	40
Larwood c Bradman b Ironmonger	8
Paynter not out	1
Voce b O'Reilly	8
Extras	32

Total 412

FALL OF WICKETS

1-7, 2-91, 3-121, 4-154, 5-245, 6-296, 7-394, 8-385, 9-403, 10-412.

AUSTRALIA—2nd innings

W. M. Woodfull not out	33
J. H. Fingleton b Larwood	0
W. H. Ponsford c Jardine b Larwood	3
D. G. Bradman c and b Verity ...	66
S. J. McCabe c Leyland b Allen ...	7
Extras	7

Total (for 4 wickets) ...116

BOWLING ANALYSIS

ENGLAND—2nd innings

	O.	M.	R.	W.
Wall	29	6	75	1
O'Reilly	50.3	21	79	4
Ironmonger ...	57	21	87	3
Grimmett	35	9	74	1
McCabe	16	0	42	0
Bradman	4	0	23	1

Byes, 17; leg-byes, 11; no-balls (Wall 2,

AMES AND VERITY SPARKL